Sell It and Scale It:

How to Transition from Salesman to CEO

By Ryan Stewman

Sell It and Scale It:

How to Transition from Salesman to CEO

ISBN-13: 978-1977908681

ISBN-10: 1977908683

Cover design by Rob Secades

Table of Contents

Chapter 1: Humble Beginnings

Sales is the only thing that has been there for me my entire life. When I say that, I mean it with 100-million-percent conviction. When times got tough, I couldn't rely on my parents, a rich relative, friend, or a company to bail me out. The only thing that ever bailed me out was sales. From a young age, I lived in a small town, and my grandfather was a banker, on my mother's side. On my father's side, my grandfather was an entrepreneur. So, my sales ability is obviously in my blood, since I come from a banking and entrepreneurial background.

In the 80s, when the S&Ls crashed, it was a horrible atrocity for our family. My entrepreneurial grandfather lost his plant. My banking grandfather lost his bank. Our family went from being social, aristocratic, popular people who owned the bank and made a bunch of money, to poor as hell and even having to leave town. It was almost as if the neighbors had run us out with pitchforks like we were witches.

My mom and I moved to a new town, and she and my father split up. Before long, I found myself in a situation where my stepdad adopted me, and I had to change my last name. Once this happened, we moved back to the same small town, and then I had to deal with all the kids asking me questions like "Why is your name different?" I would say, "I'm still the same person. My dad no longer loves me." The kids would tease me and give me a hard time, and I fucking hated school because of it.

When I finished the eighth grade, I went into high school, and then the co-op program. I got a hardship driver's license at 15 years old and went to work selling car washes at a local store for my stepfather. So, I would leave school in the ninth grade at lunch and drive to the car wash, where I would then call my stepfather (who was my adopted father), and check in. Once there; I would go sell car washes for the day. As I stood out in front of the lot, cars would pull in, and they would want a $10 wash. But they would leave with a $15 wash because it was my job to upsell them. I got paid a little commission for making those upsells.

By the end of ninth grade, I didn't have enough credits to graduate to go to the tenth grade. That meant I was set to repeat the ninth grade. I realized I was making about $25,000 a year at this car wash and that my teachers were making about the same amount of money. I also noticed that my teachers, not only made $25,000-$30,000, but I knew they had student loan debt and all sorts of other complications that I didn't have. Instead of repeating the ninth grade, I took my GED test and went to work at the car wash full-time. Because I put in more hours, my $25,000 increased to about $40,000.

While I was working at the car wash, I met one of the customers, who offered me my very first money-making scheme: moving marijuana. He would supply me with the plant, and I would supply the people who I knew smoked the shit. Just like most stories go, it was only a matter of time before we traded up the ladder, from marijuana to cocaine. In January 1999, I had been in my very first apartment for about six months, when I tried cocaine for the first time, overdosed and died. I had a seizure, and then the ambulance showed up with the shockers to bring me back to life. After that complete debacle, the police arrested me for possession of a controlled substance with intent to deliver cocaine. I was busted with roughly seven grams, or what back then was the equivalent of $200 worth of cocaine.

I woke up in the hospital chained to a bed. A police officer walked in. He'd been waiting for me. He read me my rights, and I was locked up in the county jail for three months before they finally let me out on my own recognizance. I refused to snitch, so they were looking at throwing the entire book at me. They wanted to give me as much time as possible. At one point, they offered me 20 years' probation. I wasn't even 20 years old. But I ended up taking a plea deal for two years in the state prison. My lawyer swore to me that I would only do three or four months inside the county jail, and since I was a first-time drug offender, I would make first parole. But thanks to our President, George W. Bush, the state of Texas had imposed at that time that you had to do mandatory minimum sentences on smaller sentences.

I was 18 months into a two-year stint before I made parole. I saw 9/11 happen inside the prison and the guards told us they were going to have to kill us all because we'd become enemies of the state. I've never been so scared in my life. I thought they were going to gas us in the same way that the Nazis gassed the Jewish people during World War II. The guards told us it was a possibility because there was a war on our soil. Listen, we didn't have the Internet. We didn't have access to anything other than Fox Four News, NBC Five and one other station. We were out in the middle of nowhere. No cable. No radios. No communication to the outside world other than magazines, newspapers and letters. It was the scariest time of my life.

I'll never forget the day they were going to let me go. They told me I was headed home, that I had made parole in September. I gave all my shit away after I heard that. I walked off the ring, flipped everybody the middle finger and said, "Fuck every one of you motherfuckers. You deserve to be here. I'm going home." But then they fucked up my parole and brought me back to that same unit two days later. I had to stay there for an entire month. It was the most miserable month I've ever experienced in my entire life.

After I was released from prison, I found good fortune working hard at the car wash again. I decided I'd never sell drugs ever again in my life and I haven't. I was determined that I wouldn't ever get involved in criminal activity again, and I haven't. Then I was offered a job in the mortgage industry, and I explained to the customer at the car wash, who had suggested it, that her opportunity wasn't for me. I was a convict, and I didn't know anything about mortgages. I didn't own a home. I had rented an apartment once, but then gotten kicked out of it and had gone to jail. It was just a bad idea overall; I told her after I explained everything. She replied, "If you'll come to my office, I'll teach you everything. None of what you just said matters."

I thought *well, I could wash cars and make $11 an hour plus commission or I can go try this*. She said I could get rich. Like anybody with a half a brain would, I left the car wash because I knew it would always be there and I could go back. I took the job, and within my first two months, I'd made $21,000 in mortgage commissions. I was hooked. In 2005, my gross income was $770,000. I bought cars and a nice house. But it wasn't an easy transition. The same cops in my town thought I was selling drugs again and they kicked in my door at three o'clock on a Monday, when I wasn't even home. As a matter of fact, as I pulled into the driveway, they were leaving my house because they'd figured out I wasn't in there.

I asked one of them, "Hey, what's going on?" and the police pulled me out of my truck, put guns to my head and arrested me. They had a tank outside and all sorts of shit. I was a mortgage broker. I was a loan officer. It made no sense. They said they had a warrant for drugs, that they had found drugs in my trash can, which was impossible because I hadn't even taken the trash out that week. In my home, there were no drugs, no baggies, and no scales. Nothing that would imply that anybody who lived there was doing anything illegal. But they did find a gun I had been given. In the state of Texas, you can have a gun if you're five years out of your prison sentence—and I had hit that mark when this happened.

However, the ATF has a rule superseding that law. It says, for the most part: "Ahh, we don't think so." This is the same thing that is happening with marijuana in Colorado right now. Marijuana's absolutely legal. If the sheriff pulls you over and you have marijuana in your car, you can just keep it. It's no big deal. As long as you're not high, you'll be able to drive away. But if the DEA pulls up to your dispensary and decides to raid you, you're fucked. That was the same situation with Texas, guns and felons.

Long story short, I retained a lawyer and was sentenced to 15 months federal prison time. I did my 15 months, and I came out with 25 dollars to my name. I had lost everything while inside. I had lost my wife (at the time), my savings and real estate portfolio. It was all gone. My wife left me for the landscaper. My parents and I were on bad terms. I moved into a halfway house and had to spend most of that 25 bucks on fast food because I'd been starving to death.

After a couple of months, I found a job at a mortgage place. I soon became the top producer of the largest independently owned private mortgage bank in the entire state of Texas. I closed 183 loans in 2009. But in 2010, President Obama passed a law called the Dodd-Frank Act, and it cost me my license. I had made $300,000 the previous year in gross income and had to once again face being fucked. All because yet again the federal government had gotten

12

involved in my business. I was without a job, without income. I was without money, and I didn't know what else to do to survive.

Chapter 2: Now What?

Here I was. No job. I had remarried. I hadn't seen any of it coming, so I told my then-wife, who's now an ex-wife, that she could quit her job. I had been making $300,000 a year. I knew I could take care of the two of us. She could stay at home. She could do all the things that needed to be done around the house. Then I was without a job, and she didn't want to work. She'd gotten pretty used to a comfortable life.

I made a phone call to a friend of mine, Michael Reese, and I was going to ask him for a job. Well, when Michael sat down at the table at Genghis Grill that day, he was wearing a red shirt and khaki pants. I remember it as clearly as yesterday. He told me about a seminar he'd just attended and $8,000 DVDs that he'd bought, which was mind-boggling to me because I know Mike to be one of the thriftiest people on the planet. Still, today, as I'm writing this book in 2017, Mike is driving the same vehicle he's been driving since I met him in 2003. When he mentioned he had spent $8,000 on those DVDs, I knew they must have been worth $8 million for him to make that kind of an investment because let's be real, $8,000 is a lot of money. I don't care who you are.

He said, "I want you to check these out. I think this is what you should be doing. It's something called Internet marketing." I took the DVDs home. I learned how to upload an FPS, WordPress site from a server, and I learned a bunch of coding and other stuff that thank God, we don't have to do anymore. You kids have it so easy these days. Mike's words resonated with me, which is why I watched the DVDs. He said, "Man, with your sales ability and this Internet marketing stuff, you'll get rich doing it if you just stick with it."

I created a website for an energy drink. One night, somebody bought the energy drink on autopilot. I still remember the site was called TheEnergyProducer.com. I think I still own it. Someone actually bought one of the energy drinks, and I made a commission. I even called the person up, and I was like, "Well, how did you find this? What made you decide to get involved here?" Shortly afterward, I made a mortgage product and started selling it with pay-per-click on Google. That venture made me about $30,000. It was awesome.

The next month, I took my life savings, about $20,000 at the time, on top of the $30,000 I had made, and I knew I was going to make $1M that month. But what I didn't know was that a new law had gotten passed the previous month that, since I wasn't in the mortgage business anymore, I wasn't aware of. What I had been teaching people didn't work well after all. I not only lost my advertising dollars, but I had to refund almost 80 percent of the sales I'd made because the process I'd been using wasn't legal anymore. At that moment, I had no job *again* and no money. I was broke. I'd blown all our savings. I had to face my wife at the time.

She told me she was pregnant.

I called up a friend from prison and asked if he thought it would be okay for me to work for a car dealership down the street if there was any real money it. He was a general manager and said, "Come work for my car dealership. You can make way more money." I went to work in car sales, and thought, *well, that's a logical flip to go from mortgages to car sales. I'm sure they're a lot alike.* Boy, was I wrong. In the mortgage world, you make $300,000. You work 40 hours a week, and life is good. In the car world, you make $80,000. You work 80 hours a week, and everybody's miserable around you. At least that was my experience.

But, I still became the top producer. I sold more cars than anybody else, but I also did a lot of half deals because I didn't like the hours. I was top producer for about six months, and when my son, Jax was born, I quit immediately. I'd only worked there to make sure I had a little bit of money and some insurance in case something went wrong with the pregnancy and birth. As soon as we received a healthy diagnosis, I quit.

While I was at the car dealership in 2011, I tested some of my social media marketing theories. I sent videos to clients showing them cars, and telling them how to get to the office. I introduced myself on these videos. It was powerful, and that's why I sold so many cars. I had plugged my Internet marketing system into the car dealership, and it was working.

I left the car dealership and started my own company called Postfuser with two business partners. I wrote three posts a day for three social media channels. If you had a Facebook, LinkedIn and Twitter, I would write three posts and upload them into Hootsuite, which automatically schedules your posts. I had about 70 clients at one time, so you can imagine 70 times three. That means I was writing 210 posts a day I had to load into Hootsuite. Sure, I had a nice little system that made my job easier, but it also drove everybody nuts.

My two business partners quit. They took off with a lot of money, which sentenced me to working even harder. I was stuck making a hundred bucks a month for 70 people, which was about $7,000. I still had to pay staff. It was ridiculous, so I stopped. At that moment, I said, "I'm going to start teaching people *how* to do this. I have the experience now. I've run social media for 70 people. I've run social media through a dealership. I've used social media in the mortgage business. I'm going to start teaching people this strategy because it's a huge market that nobody understands." In 2011 and 2012, there was literally nobody in the field. It was unheard of. Now, everybody knows social media is the way to go. Back then, when I would tell people about what I was doing, they would say, "You mean the Facebook for my friends?"

Sure, I was making 70 sales. Sure, I was the top producer in the car business, which meant between $8,000-$10,000 a month. But I was out of money again. I had gotten used to making 30 grand a month, so 8 to 10 grand a month was like the tax bill I had paid when I was at the top of my game. That kind of money didn't get me out of debt. It didn't allow me to have an extravagant lifestyle because it was less than what I'd been earning. You might think, *dude, 80 grand a year, 150 grand a year, that's a lot of money*. It wasn't to me.

Here I was free as a bird. No longer locked up, and I was moving in with my in-laws. Don't cry for me, because luckily, my in-laws lived in a very nice house. It was about 8,000 square feet, so my wife and I at the time could use the bedrooms upstairs. We weren't cramped in a trailer in the middle of West Texas somewhere. But at the same time, it was humbling to go from being a person right on the cusp of making a million per year to living with my parents. Can you imagine the strain that caused the relationship? The pain that caused my ego? But there I was, recording videos from my in-laws' house telling my story. You can still watch those videos on YouTube today. When you check it out, you'll see I've kept it real this whole time. My videos are essentially like: "I fucked up, but I'm not giving up, but I definitely fucked up," Even with all the events from my past, I've never fucked *anybody over*.

I always use my own money. I always use my own experience, my own stuff, and I've always taken personal responsibility. At that point, I had to do something because I was tired of writing 210 posts a day and living with my in-laws. Something had to give.

Chapter 3: Little Old Lady Closers

While I was managing social media, most of my clients were real estate agents. Then I connected with a title company, and the title company let me have a little office in the back of their building. They didn't charge me any rent. They just wanted me to send them referrals. They knew I had a lot of realtors I could introduce them to, and they wanted me to use their spot to conduct social media trainings, so it was mutually beneficial. I would get realtors into their office, and train them, and they would network with them for their business. This was a clever arrangement because I got free rent and could also sell to realtors.

Well, this office had a few ladies who were older, in their late 60s or 70s. You know, the blue hairs. Not to be misogynist or sexist or anything, but they were little old ladies with blue hair running around. That's who this particular title company liked to hire. What struck me about that was the fact their business card would say "Closers." You would read: "Peggy Smith, Closer." "Myrtle Smith, Closer."

One day, a friend and I were knocking back a few Coronas in the office when one of the ladies came by. She wrote down a note for me on the back of her card. I guess somebody had stopped by, or I had missed a call. My friend said, "Look at her card. It says Closer." My friend was a salesperson from the mortgage business, too. To us, in the car business and mortgage business, a closer was somebody who was a good salesperson.

It was funny to us that these little, old blue-haired ladies were closers. I was like, "Yeah, man. They're hardcore closers." We were having a good laugh about it, but then I went to GoDaddy and looked up the domain HardcoreCloser.com, thinking, *that's actually a really cool sounding name. I'm going to register it.* Sure enough, I bought it. Remember that $8,000 DVD course? I used my knowledge from that course to upload my very first blog to HardcoreCloser.com.

As you know, the vision for Hardcore Closer today is completely different than when I first started the company. Back then, I just needed a place to house my YouTube videos. I thought, *well, if I'm going to coach loan officers and real estate agents on how to use social media to get business like I've done, then I'm going to need a website to host the videos.* That's why HardcoreCloser.com was invented. While I was at the title company, loan officers and real estate agents would come over, and I would shoot videos with them, while I said something like, "Hey, this is Ryan Stewman, real estate agent in xyz neighborhood, and I'm excited to talk to you about your property. Reach out to me at the number below." These were little, simple 30-second clip videos, and I needed a website where I could embed them.

Well, suddenly, after I'd recorded 10 to 15 different real estate agents, and 10 to 15 loan officers, and after I had loaded up a bunch of videos and content on the blog from other people, the people I had featured started showing their friends the examples. They'd say, "Here's how we're doing. Look, my content is on this website. This is how we give out our information." Then their friends would come to me wanting to do the same, and so on and so forth.

Somewhere along the way, people started calling me the Hardcore Closer. They're like, "It's the Hardcore Closer guy." "Yeah, what's up, Closer?" That wasn't really my intention with the project. My intention was to simply have a website. I'm also smart enough to know that, if someone gives you a cool nickname, you run with it. If you get a shitty nickname, you may never shake it off. I was like, *Hardcore Closer, that's a sweet nickname, I'll go with that.*

As I shared more and more of these videos, I noticed if I had drinks somewhere in Dallas, for example, people would know me out of the blue, like I was some kind of star. "I watch the videos you guys upload on there. That's really cool." After about the third or fourth time of being recognized, I decided to get to super serious. I bought a book on writing called *Kick-Ass Copywriting Secrets of a Marketing Rebel* by John Carlton. I do recommend that you buy the book, too. I bought how-to-write-email books from Ben Settle and the late and great Scott Haines. I wanted to become the best writer that I could, so I could make better videos and then write better blog posts. If the blog took off by accident, I could send people to it and list more product. It would be a place to acquire more realtors and loan officers, a place to keep a personal journey of my sales knowledge and experience.

That was in 2012. Here we are in 2017, and that website produces seven figures a year in income. Just last month alone, as I'm writing this book, 2,012 leads came from that website. It's been that way for years now. Learning to write was one of the greatest things I ever did. I have always been a good face-to-face salesperson. I learned that at the carwash. Someone pulled up, rolled their window down, and I looked them in the eye and made a sale. I'd always been good on the phone. I would pick up the phone, make the cold or warm call, the inbound or outbound lead; it didn't matter. I was always good at it. I can get up in a room full of people and talk. I was always a natural at that, too. But, I hadn't had any practice persuading people with my writing.

I knew if I was going to become a master salesperson, I was going to have to treat sales like martial arts. People who are master MMA, mixed martial arts, who know karate, jiu-jitsu, grappling, or wrestling are experts in a multitude of areas. They can fight in any style. I thought *I want to do the same thing with sales. I want to sell in any style.*

If you meet me face-to-face, I can close you. If you meet me on the phone, I can close you. If you meet me in a webinar, I can close you. Guess what I can also do? I can close you through my emails. I can close you through my text messages. I can close you through direct messages. Writing changed my life, and if this were martial arts, that blog has been my dojo, the place where I go to practice. The place where I grapple with words. As of today, in 2017, I've written over 1,000 articles. I've produced over 1,400 videos on YouTube. I've learned to sell and become a master salesperson across all platforms because that's my identity: a salesperson. And it all started with an investment.

Chapter 4: This Shit is Not for Me

Here I was with my website, and a blog people were paying attention to, as well as a social media company with 70 clients. I was writing 210 posts a day, and I'd had enough. I could not continue to do the work, and I couldn't continue to keep the 70 clients I had plus take the time to train anyone new, so I was between what you would call a rock and a hard place.

I was "proper fucked" as they say over in England. I had to figure out a way to put an end to the shit. I was sick of it. It wasn't for me. I had honed my writing skills, and I enjoyed writing, but I didn't like writing social media posts for everybody else, and plus, as I was writing these social media posts I would see real estate agents making $5,000 and $10,000 per sale from the content I'd generated for them…all the while I sat there earning 100 bucks a month.

As I said, I didn't have a whole lot of money, but I remembered hearing about a guy named Frank Kern on one of the DVDs in the $8,000 program that Michael Reese had shared with me. Frank Kern ran a webinar with a gentleman named Kevin Nations. The course they were selling at the time was also coincidentally $8,000.

I didn't have $8,000 then. I was on my last leg living with my in-laws. I was exhausted from my fucking life, so I hustled up $8,000. And I can't remember exactly where it came from, but I probably borrowed it from the in-laws, maybe sold a couple more social media deals, maybe did training for a real estate company. There's no telling what I did, but I got busy, and within 48 hours, I came up with the $8,000.

It's amazing what can happen when you put your mind to it, and you decide you really want something. I reached out to Dr. Kern and Kevin Nations, paid them the $8,000 and they taught me a 12-week course. The course took place twice weekly. I was there religiously. I knew if I invested the $8,000 it *had* to change my life because it was all I had.

I invested in the program and turned my situation around within a couple of days to sign up two new people at $1,000 a month. Then I signed up two more people at

$1,000 a month. And then I sold two more people on committing to a year upfront. They gave me $10,000. Suddenly, I'd made more than my $8,000 back. I paid back the people I had borrowed the money from, and I also kept some for myself. About a month after the program, Kevin Nations reached out to me and said, "Would you like to join my mastermind for $25,000?"

I thought, *well fuck, I didn't have eight before. I don't have 25 now. Fuck it. Yeah, sure. Why not?* So, I put more pressure on myself to come up with 25 grand, which took me about five months. I paid it off at $5,000 a month for another five months. Then I went out to Kevin Nations' house, and he taught me how to make big money from the small events process he used. I had learned all about the online coaching programs from the $8,000 product; then I was also able to implement the knowledge I had soaked up about how to earn "Big Money From Small Events" from the $25,000 mastermind.

I gathered all the information and learned how to apply it to my business, which led me to create a program called The Tribe. Instead of making $100 a month per person, I wanted to make $10,000 per person and only work with a few people. If I did that, I could make $300,000 a year. It was simple math. I just picked 30 people at $10,000 per year. Thirty prospects don't require a lot over the course of a year. It works out to be less than three people a month.

Overall, The Tribe seemed like a great way to make things happen. I followed exactly what Kevin Nations taught me. Then I launched The Tribe mastermind. It started off as a group just for loan officers. Because I'm the type of person who believes in staying in my own lane, I didn't want to teach what I didn't know. Besides, I've made fun of all my college friends for going to college to learn from some motherfucker who has no real-world experience.

I didn't want to be that motherfucker. When I spoke on topics, I wanted them to be from my personal experience, so nobody could form a weapon of doubt against me. Naturally, the first thing I taught was social media marketing for loan officers because that's what I had done. I had been one of the best single-person operation loan officers on the planet in one of the worst years to fucking have that job from 2008 to 2010. I had generated a ton of leads for myself as well as a ton of leads for the real estate agents I worked with while I was in the Postfuser phase.

I had gained an immense amount of experience rapidly because I'd run social media for 70 different loan officers and real estate agents and I understood how the market worked. So, I started taking on loan officers and teaching them how to do what I had done. I taught them what agents truly wanted, how to generate leads and how to hold workshops agents would actually attend.

Instead of talking about interest rates and boring-ass mortgage programs, my loan officers would go into their company meeting and talk about how to generate listing leads, which is what a fucking agent wants anyway, and mortgages would be the *byproduct* of that. It worked. It worked in such a major way that the first three people who signed up said this: "I don't know who the fuck you are, and I've never given $10,000 to anybody in my life, but you sound like you know what the fuck you're talking about."

Steve Green, Brandin Scharlin and TJ Barker were the first three people to ever fucking take a chance on me. I know for a fact those three guys' lives have changed as a result. I see them on Facebook all the time. Here's what I want you to think about. In the midst of a shitty situation, in the midst of something I was sick and tired of being a part of, I discovered the shit I was doing wasn't for me. I was living with my in-laws. I had zero money saved up. I had zero money in my bank account.

Somehow, I still found the money to invest in myself. I still used what I had learned, and I created a program, which you'll later learn would go on to earn millions upon millions of dollars. At the same time, the struggle wasn't over yet because I'd gotten three clients in the first month. The struggle had just begun.

Chapter 5: My First Digital Program

Although I had sold these three loan officers into my program and they were getting results, the problem was I wasn't protected against loss of money if one of them were to drop out. I would lose one-third of my income if they didn't pay 10 grand one month. They agreed to pay about $750 a month for 12 months while they were involved. So, even though there was a contract in place, it was about as firm as a handshake. I knew I had to get side money rolling. Plus, I had been recording all the training I'd done for the loan officers; and I thought *I could just resell some of these trainings. I could package them up.* That's when it hit me; *I have the ultimate digital product.*

I was going to teach loan officers how to pay for title policies for builders in exchange for the builder's business. If you're a loan officer, all you're trying to do is sell mortgages on homes. If you're a builder, all you're trying to do is sell homes for the maximum amount of profit possible. When I was a loan officer, if you made $5,000 in commissions, you could pay that money toward a title policy. Let's say a title policy might be $2,000 and you made $5,000. I would be willing to risk $2,000 to make $3,000 all the time. Instead of making five grand, I only made three grand, but in my mind, three grand was better than no grand. I did this a lot when I was a loan officer.

The Dodd-Frank Act had caused me to lose my mortgage license, so at this time, I was almost three years into not working in the mortgage business. I didn't realize what I was teaching had become illegal. I was teaching loan officers how they could go out and buy the title insurance from the builders, and I wasn't telling them that's what I was selling in the advertisements. Put it another way; I was teaching loan officers how to get business from builders through a process that had become obsolete and illegal. This, in turn, caused them a massive, massive influx of refunds.

As I mentioned in the previous chapter, I had invested about $50,000, lost it all, and then some. I was in serious trouble. I didn't know where my next meal was coming from. If my in-laws hadn't cooked, I would have starved. Yet, I knew what I had been working on was possible because I had made sales. Yes, the program failed, and I had to refund it because I had made mistakes due to lack of knowledge. But I still knew the potential was out there, and so I immediately created another product called the Facebook Syndicate.

We sold memberships into the Facebook Syndicate for 400 bucks, and they were going like hotcakes. I sold 100 in my first two weeks. Then Facebook sent me an email that said, "Facebook is a registered trademark, and you cannot use Facebook or have a domain with the word Facebook in it, or you're in direct violation of our copyright, trademark," and all sorts of other regulations. I switched the name of the program from the Facebook Syndicate to the Social Media Syndicate due to the cease and desist.

Doing this was a little more complicated than you might think because I had written all my ads, my whole campaign, my logos, everything around the Facebook Syndicate. And all of it had to be changed. I had to buy the Social Media Syndicate site from somebody else since they had created it while I had made the Facebook Syndicate. Remember, this was in 2012-2013 when Facebook was new territory for everyone.

To recap. Yes, I had failed with a digital product for loan officers. But I'd resiliently turned around and created another product for real estate agents and loan officers that used social media and had nothing to do with title work, but was obsolete and illegal. Then out of nowhere, Facebook sent me a cease and desist, so I had to rebrand my whole Facebook Syndicate program to the Social Media Syndicate, and just when it had been flying off the shelf! I was bashing my head against the wall. If I were a religious person, I would have said a prayer like this, "God, I have been your humble, faithful servant. Every time I seem to get ahead, you fucking step on me like a roach. What in the fuck is the deal?" But instead, I just put my head down and went back to work.

I remembered the trainings from the three loan officers who were my clients, and that I had another 6-12 weeks' worth of trainings I had recorded as well. I took the trainings and packaged them up. Again, I went back to the drawing board and used all new logos, a brand-new sales page; all new videos; and an all-new launch sequence inside a platform called Kajabi. Supercharged Production was born.

Supercharged Production allowed me to sell loan officers a $200 program branded just for them that would teach them how to market themselves on Facebook. I sold about 50 in my first month. It wasn't a bad living. It produced some residual income alongside the three loan officers who were still my clients. From there, I created another digital product called Magnetic Media for $27. The idea was to give people a taste of what was possible. I had no problems with this offering at all.

The secret was in the $27 Magnetic Media package. This service had some of our top content because we wanted to put our best foot forward, so you would you think, *well, if that's what you get for $27, imagine what you get for $200.* Magnetic Media sold thousands of copies within its first year. At that point, and again, faster than I had expected, a few loan officers traded up from the Supercharged Production program. They were like, "We paid the 200 bucks and the shit works. What do we have to do to maybe work with you?"

I took on more people.

Then it hit me (again). I had low-end products leading the way to my digital products. That realization changed the game for me. I knew at that moment; I could create one-off income and residual income. I could pair them together. With that goal at the forefront of my mind, I took off for Kevin Nations' house in Nevada for the second time.

Chapter 6: BFA Live is Born

I flew out to Nevada, and it was nerve-wracking because I had used my last dollar. I'd invested in Kevin's program, made a little bit of money and then invested more money. I've always been an investor. When you're going to grow a business, you can't just collect money and sit on it. You must put that money to work for you. I learned that in the drug game. Once you run out of product, you have to buy more product. Then, you need to sell it, and…again you buy more product and sell it.

The same thing applies to business. You've got to buy more ads. You've got to put more technology to work. You've got to buy more websites, and on it goes. But there I was, on my last dollar. I arrived at Kevin's beautiful mansion in Nevada for his mastermind and met AJ Roberts, Garret J. White, Jodi Jelas, Setema Gali, Brian Horn and a ton of other badass players. Then there was me. The brokest person in the room. The one newest to everything they were teaching, but I was so hungry. It was unreal. I was starving, and I would've done anything because if I didn't, I would be stuck in Nevada.

Literally, I had spent my last dollar to get there, and if I didn't make a dollar at the mastermind, I would be in big-ass trouble. I would have to pay for the hotel room with money I didn't have. At the time, I didn't carry credit cards because I was scared I would run up a charge on them and end up owing money, so I avoided them altogether. If I didn't get money in my PayPal card account ASAP, I would be in a major bind.

When I walked into the room, Kevin said, "Ryan, what do you need help with?" I replied, "I need leads." He said, "Let me introduce you to AJ Roberts." AJ brought me over to where he was set up and said, "I'm going to show you how to run something called Facebook ads." I told him, "I've been running Facebook ads for a while." He goes, "I'll show you how to do it the right way."

We sat down at the computer and started running a funnel. We took a video from my YouTube account and uploaded it to Facebook. In that video, I was recorded as simply saying, "If you sell two million dollars or less a month in mortgages, and you'd like help bypassing that two million-dollar monthly mark, fill out this form. We'll get on the phone, and I'll teach you the strategy that will have real estate agents chasing you down, practically beating you with their clients."

We attached a Wufoo form to it. The Wufoo form asked a few questions: "What's your production?" "How much money do you make a month?" "How many realtors do you work with?" And so on and so forth. We posted that simple video with the Wufoo link, then wrote a small bit of copy for loan officers that said: "Attention loan officers, if you don't do $2 million a month, then let us help you out." We ran an ad to it and targeted a few well-known mortgage coaches.

We knew that other mortgage coaches had successful pages on Facebook, so we targeted their pages. Then we went to lunch and thank God, Kevin paid because I didn't have enough money to cover my part of the bill. But I was famished and willing to risk it. I had planned on blaming the fact I couldn't pay on traveling. If the money wasn't there, I would say, "It must be because I'm on the road, I'll call them when I get back to Kevin's house. Can somebody cover me? I'll get you back."

But, while we were sitting at lunch, leads flooded in. "Bing! Bing! Bing!" My phone went off left and right with lead after lead. I looked down, and within a matter of 15 or 20 minutes, I had 20 leads. Within another 5 or 10 minutes, I had another 5 or 6 leads; they were coming in sometimes two or three a minute. My phone loaded up with leads. So, I excused myself from the living room as soon as we got back to Kevin's house, and went down into his basement. I made sales calls and sold $10,000 worth of product in about two hours. This money was paid to me immediately, just sent right to my PayPal account, so I could pay my hotel and food bills for the night. We had a good time in Vegas that night because I was celebrating a victory.

When I came back from Kevin's house two days later, I started to bankroll. I was successful. Ads were going gangbusters. I was charging $1,000 for a month membership in The Tribe. When I sat down at Kevin's house with four or five other super-influential, super-important people he taught me how to do something called "Big Money From Small Events." Kevin basically said, "Look, you guys all paid $25,000 to be here at my house for two days. Would you like to know how you could charge people to come to your house for two days, so they can learn from your expertise?" Obviously, when you hear those words, you have an "aha" moment like, *it worked for him. It'll work for me.*

That's when we started designing a small business workshop that was more than a seminar called "Break Free Academy." A person could come in with no knowledge of how to market whatsoever. They could learn social media marketing on day one and by day two, could leave the event with funnels in place, Facebook ads running, Google ads running, or whatever else they needed to do. People didn't just learn the stuff only to figure out how to implement it on their own. That's the worst thing about seminars. You go to a seminar, pick up a bunch of knowledge but come Monday you are in charge of doing it by yourself.

I wanted people to come to the workshop, to learn what they needed to and leave with everything done, so they could get on with their life. That's when we created Break Free Academy. The event has grown significantly from the very first event that had about three people to (as of this writing), selling out at 75 people per event at $5,000 per person. We have 80 attendees coming to the next one. Somebody's gonna be standing up.

Chapter 7: Divorce on the Horizon

As you can probably guess, my life has been filled with ups and downs. Every time it seems like I reach a pinnacle, I hit a divot and end up in a valley. Matter of fact, my life has not been a series of ups and downs. It's been a series of rocket ships and submarines.

I left Nevada on a rocket ship to come home and sell people into The Tribe and into the new workshop, Break Free Academy. We were selling people into our live event, too. For the third event, 10 people showed up. When I came home from the event, I looked at some flip houses in South Dallas. By the time I got back to my house after Break Free Academy and looking at those flip houses, my house was empty. My then-wife had decided she'd had enough of the ups and downs. Listen, it's no shame to her. She married a guy who had a W-2 sales job and made 300 grand a year. He had gone to church, but then he had turned into a different person. I was self-employed. I was true to myself. I was no longer a fake person. It was a lot for her to handle.

When I got home, literally, all my shit was gone, I was in one of the biggest shit storms of my life. I had to move out of my house. I didn't have a lot of money because I'd invested it all back into my business. I had to pay all her bills because she was a stay-at-home mom, which meant I had to *pay all her bills on top of paying all my bills.* I had to pay for the house until we sold it, and then I had to move out of that house and rent somewhere else because I couldn't buy anything while we were married. It was a fucking nightmare, to put it lightly.

On top of that, I was dealing with a battle for child custody and pretty much everything else that you can think of, trying to run a business, trying to survive divorce. It was like a video game with all those challenges coming at me. In a video game, the level itself is pretty hard, but when you get to the big boss at the end, you have to work like a madman to beat that big boss and get promoted to the next level. At that time in my life, all the challenges coming at me were the big boss.

About a year into trying to get a divorce, I got a phone call from my attorney, who said, "I've got some good news for you." First of all, my attorney was a dipshit, and I should have never hired the guy, but I was already committed, so I was just letting it roll. Later, I would end up getting the divorce finalized by firing my attorney. Imagine that. He called me, saying, "I talked to your wife's attorney, and we had your businesses evaluated. It turns out they're worthless, so she doesn't want any part of them. Matter of fact, she can't have any part of them. Here's the thing, Mr. Stewman. If you were to pass away tomorrow, if you got hurt on your motorcycle or if you were in a car wreck or something of that nature, then your business would go away. You don't have a sustainable business. You have a consulting business that requires 100 percent of your attention. If you don't give it that attention, it disappears."

While on the one hand, I was glad I wouldn't have to share equity in the companies I had built with my ex-wife, on the other hand, it felt like I had been slapped in the face because my life's work was useless. That's when I knew I had to make adjustments. I had to start changing the way I had done business because what had gotten me to that point wouldn't continue to carry me to where I wanted to go. I had to come up with a new start. Sure, they were worthless businesses, but I was making money, probably $20,000 a month at the time I got that news. Of course, I was investing $19,000 of it back into bills and to grow the company. If I had died, nobody would have paid me because my business was 100 percent based on me showing up. If I didn't show up, then I didn't get to do business.

So, I started creating digital products I could sell on autopilot through email that didn't require me to physically be there to teach an event. I wasn't required to physically be present to educate and consult clients in my Tribe. Instead, I could use some of the material I had created over the years from teaching and showing up at events. I could utilize every bit of knowledge I had gained. I put it all together to create digital content, sent out emails and ran ads to the digital content. A person would purchase the product; then they would get their log-in instructions. The whole process was executed on autopilot. In other words, I didn't have to do anything.

As you can guess, I could only do this for a certain amount of time before it got out of hand as well. I realized it would be better for me to start scaling my business and to no longer be the one-man show. Kevin Nations runs a one-man business called The Family. I went to Anthem in Las Vegas and met with him. This is "Big Money From Small Events" put into play. It's a tight-knit circle of entrepreneurs who pay him, and he does 100 percent of the work himself. He doesn't have anybody who works for him. That was the model I was going to top, but then I realized I have different goals than Mr. Nations. I have bigger expectations of myself.

If I was going to reach the 300 million people I had set as a target, then I was going to need a system that was bigger than just me. I was going to have to scale a team. I had gotten a fresh, new start with my digital products, but I was about to start hiring salespeople and training those salespeople in how to take over and sell my digital products, too. It was cool that I had been training clients for years. I had taught them how to market, sell and follow-up. But I had never trained an employee in any of those skills, which is completely different. To teach somebody your personal systems, so they will replicate you versus teaching somebody a new system designed for their business, the process and the objectives are night and day.

It wouldn't be long before Roxanne Hoover asked me for a job to be my first salesperson. Her husband had been a client of mine for about a year at that time. While I was reluctant at first, I'm sure glad I ended up letting her in because she opened my eyes to a whole new world and started up an entirely different revenue stream with me.

Chapter 8: Straight-Up Sales Beast

Even though I hired Roxanne to make sales for me, there was no way on God's green Earth I was going to turn her loose onto my entire company to put everything and all my fate into her hands. It wasn't going to happen. I had to do two things: level up and train Roxanne on how to sell my products, and I had to work harder because while I was training her, I wouldn't make any of my own sales. That meant I was not only training her in how to make sales, but I had to make sales myself. I was doing double the work. Lindsay, my assistant, had been with me for two years and she had to double her workload, too, because she had to get everybody set up.

My company is Hardcore Closer. I had to be the Hardcore Closer. I had to be the example, the leader; the person people talked to when they called. They would either get me or one of my salespeople, I decided. Regardless I had to ensure whoever answered had the chops and the professionalism to handle the call. My clients needed that experience, so they could say, "You know what? I want to be like that person." Or, "You know what? I want my salespeople to be like that person." I couldn't put myself or my team in a position to fail the community, not with a name like Hardcore Closer. Failure wasn't going to happen on my watch.

As I ramped up, I realized my entire identity is that of a salesperson. I had this epiphany that if I were going to build a real company, if I were going to leave a legacy for my kids, if I were going to get anywhere near reaching the goals I had set for myself, I would have to shake that identity as a salesperson and take on a new identity as a CEO. My struggle was the sales aspect. It had been the one thing that had been there for me my entire life. It was the only thing I could ever depend on.

Going through a divorce? *I'll just make some sales. It'll be all right.* Going to prison? *It's okay; when you get out, just make a bunch of sales. Make up for lost time.* Oh, your parents kicked you out of the house? Oh, you ran away from home? *Go make some sales.* I learned that no matter what situation I faced in life, I could rely on sales to get me out of it. You don't have enough money for a lawyer? *Just make some sales, and then pay him.* Your wife's taking all your money, and you're getting a divorce? You've got to find a new place to live? *Better go make more sales.* That answer was all I had ever needed my entire life, and it was all anybody had ever known of me as a young man and even a little kid. When I was five or six years old, people would remark, "He's going to grow up to be a salesman." They say the same thing about my oldest son, Jax now. "He's going to be a closer."

But my schedule was to the point of no return. There weren't enough hours in the day. I wasn't enjoying life. I wasn't enjoying the fruits of my labor. I would wake up at 4 AM and go to sleep at midnight and then wake up again the next day at 4 AM, and then go to sleep at midnight. I had calls all day, emails all night, clients in different countries. I was trying to train Roxanne. Then I brought on a guy named Johnny Ringold. So, my schedule changed again. I was struggling to train Johnny, getting him up to speed, but every time I made progress, and we were almost there, I had to let go of the reins. When I loosened my grip, I let go of my identity, too, because the reins I had at that time were sales. If I let go of sales, that meant I was letting go of me.

Sales was my whole existence, the building block of my entire company and life.

But I was exhausted. There wasn't any coming back from my plans. There weren't any days off. While I was going through my divorce, my son would come over to my penthouse, and we wouldn't have time to play. We wouldn't get to spend as much quality time as I wanted together, and I didn't feel like I was living up to be the dad I'd never had. The dad I'd always promised him I would be. I was dead on my feet, and I had to do something to scale the business.

While Roxanne and Johnny wound up sticking around for a while, three or four people I had trained quit. I realized these salespeople were, in fact, showing up to get training from me and then leaving to start their own job or they were taking advantage of whatever their own dreams were, using my training. I didn't catch on until about the fifth one left me. Then I thought, *I'm training these fucks for free and giving them skills I would normally charge a lot of money for, and they're just taking off and going back to work.*

I knew if I was going to reach the amount of people I wanted to, if I was going to give the impact to the world I aimed to give, I had to keep hiring. So, what if they got over on me? So, what if guys came on board and then left?

I was a straight-up sales beast. It was my thing, and I couldn't let it go. I'd be on a sales call with somebody and closing two other people via chat. Then I'd record a video right after that of me closing more people before sending it off to Johnny and Roxanne and the rest of the team who were selling for us. I had to hand off the materials and trainings to my salespeople to get them tuned up. If I wanted my sales team to turn into sales beasts, I had to be the ultimate sales beast.

Again, I was facing that big boss at the end of the level, because salespeople were quitting on me. There was no more time. I was missing out on my son, and everything in between. If I just pushed through to the next level, life and business would be so much sweeter.

Chapter 9: The Solo Scale-Up

I had a couple of salespeople and admins working for me at this stage in the game, but I was still a salesman. Every day, I was taking messages and writing my own emails. I was responding to emails people sent me and to direct messages on the Hardcore Closer page, the Break Free Academy page, and my Ryan Stewman personal profile. That was on top of the tweets, the LinkedIn messages, the Instagram messages, Snapchat photos and every other form of communication. I was bombarded. Every. Single. Day. As soon as I woke up, I would get on the computer. Then I would answer all the emails and DMs that had come in the night before. Once that was done, I would hit the gym and let my frustrations out.

I was up before dawn, prospecting and being proactive so I could get my exercise done. By the time I sat back down at the laptop again, it was about 7:30 or 8:30 in the morning and responses were already piling up, which would keep me reacting all day long. I was coaching people on one phone call a week, too. Folks were paying $10,000 a year to be a part of our Tribe coaching program, and I was spending an hour per week with each one of those members.

If you think about it, 15 or 20 clients, made up 20 of my 60 work hours, not the before and after portion, but the nine to five portion. I was, in essence, repeating myself over and over and over again on these calls. I knew it wasn't a sustainable system. Because how could I scale to 100 clients when I only had a certain number of hours to use? How was I going to handle that? To reach my goal, I needed to make money from 100 clients, but there was no way I could scale my business working 100 hours a week. There was also no way I was going to pass it off to somebody else and have them become a certified Hardcore Closer coach when I didn't have anybody who could fit that description right then.

I had to make the shift. Once we got to about 20 people in The Tribe, I started doing group trainings instead of one-on-one calls. I still do the group calls to this day. Now, we have 114 people who are in The Tribe. The membership is $30,000 a year, and every class is a group setting. Every

Monday, we have a group call. Every Thursday, we have a group webinar. If Tribe members need me in between, yes, they can reach out to me, but I don't spend my hours upon hours upon hours in exchange for dollars promised anymore. My salespeople had added more people, and the scale-up was inevitable, but I was still wrapping my arms around the group system.

I had to piss a few people off. You have to break a few eggs to make an omelet. I had to change the rules on a couple of people, and what happens with change is that it's going to happen with or without you, but it'll probably piss you off first. A lot of processes were switched up because we had grown to where instead of me selling somebody and them knowing me by the time we got on the phone, I was talking to complete strangers who had given me $5,000, $10,000, $15,000, $20,000, even $30,000. We ramped up to 40 people in The Tribe at $25,000 a year. I was doing the group settings, and everything worked well. That's when I introduced events.

Break Free Academy is a two-day live workshop where you pay $5,000, and you can arrive with zero experience or assets, but you will leave with leads. That's the whole intention. You learn how to do it; you build it, and you leave with your funnels and everything we teach you already done. It's not a "come and 'rah, rah,' feel good. Learn a bunch of stuff and then go to work Monday and get it done" program. So, while I'd always invited The Tribe members to those programs and those events, we had grown The Tribe large enough to where we needed to have our own events. I still had to run Break Free Academy events, but I started filling out six events a year: four Break Free Academies and two Tribe events. This was on top of coaching people because, at the time, I was also running that offering through the Break Free Academy.

I was still offering 90 days coaching with the people who'd gone through the Break Free Academy. But by the time that cycle ended, the next one was firing up, and it was just a never-ending struggle. I learned from all those group events how to leverage my services, and I learned how to start training and find leaders within the group. Sure, as had happened when I hired salespeople, I made a few mistakes, but I also learned that to be a great leader you have to raise up other leaders.

I was looking for people who had attended three or four of these events because to my mind, one day they would train at these events as well. Salespeople were loading me down with work, so I had to make massive pivots and shifts.

I might've sold a membership to one person three months ago with the understanding we would get on a call once a week for an hour. But that wasn't a sustainable plan anymore. Not with 40 people. So, I had to go back to that person and sell them on staying with me, even though they would not be getting the hour they had been promised in the beginning. Like anything else, if you're going to move and grow, you must face the big boss at the end before you can get to the next level.

Chapter 10: The Time Crunch

There comes a time in every entrepreneur's life where you realize there just aren't enough hours in the day to accomplish what you've set out to do. No matter how hard you work and no matter how many hours you put in, it seems as if you're always starting back over from square one and always running behind. One thing I've known over the years...and I've watched tons of entrepreneurs, and business owners face...there's a tipping point in life.

Let me be clear. For successful people, there is a tipping point in life. What happens at that tipping point is suddenly, a decision is made that you will no longer trade your time for dollars. That's what you do in the beginning. You trade your time for dollars. When I started using social media, I didn't have dollars, so I spent time on the site for dollars. I would post, was active in groups and prospected. I would do my Lucky Seven method and everything else I needed to do to stay on track.

When I started making money, I shifted my mindset for paying dollars for time. See, at the beginning of the workman's history, whether you're a salesman, entrepreneur, or a business owner, whatever, it does not matter, you'll trade your time for dollars. As you become more successful, you'll move up the ladder. When that happens, you will transition to trading your dollars for someone else's time.

In my case, working on Facebook in the early stages and then ultimately paying out so I didn't have to stay on the site as often was absolutely a blessing because you don't want to stay on Facebook any longer than necessary. When I worked Facebook, I traded my time for dollars. I amassed a good book of clients. Quite a few people wanted to do business with me and ended up doing business with me. Suddenly, I found myself in a situation where I had more clients than I had time, and there were not enough hours in my life.

Now, listen. Anytime you have a business with too many clients, you probably think, *well, this poor schmuck's complaining about making a bunch of money.* But here's what really happens. If you have many clients, and you can't fulfill the service that you promised those clients, which is the reason they became clients in the first place, they will lash out against you. They will leave bad reviews on Yelp. They will talk about how they spent money with you, and how their experience sucked. That's the last thing any of us want as a salesperson or a business person.

Many times, when people come to me and say, "I want to learn more about marketing and sales," I'll say, "What are you going to do if you get 100 new clients in today?" There have only been maybe five people in the history of me doing this who have said, "If I get 100 clients, then they will just fall into our system." Most people say, "I couldn't handle 100 clients." If you were a single realtor or a single loan officer and 100 applications fell into your lap, you likely couldn't get through all of them this month alone. Not by yourself.

What do you do? In a flash, you'd find yourself in a situation where you're paying for somebody else's time. It happens. I was in a situation where I didn't have enough hours in the day anymore. I had too many clients, and in the business world, that's called maxed out. That was it for me. I was at my peak earning potential. We get into sales because we want no glass ceiling and an unlimited income potential. We are salespeople, and because there is no cap on our income (except in this situation), I was capped. For the first time in my life, I was capped. You see, in the past, I've been capped, too, but I hadn't been intelligent and experienced enough to realize I had been capped. Well, at this point in my journey, I was capped. I was capped on time. I was capped on clients, and the worst part of it all was that I was capped on income as well.

What do you do when you find yourself in an ultimate time crunch? I started waking up earlier and going to sleep later, but all that did was take away from me. Yes, I am not a me-first guy. I am a you-first guy. I am a servant. I am a servant-leader. I am a person who serves those who trust me with their business. I'm the one who serves those who trust me with their respect and their compassion and their love as friends and family. That's what I do, serve people. That's my purpose here on this planet, and I was out of time to serve. I had more people than I could serve in the amount of time at my disposal.

You realize an epiphany when you go through a time crunch like that. You recognize *I'm maxed out. For the first time in my life, the only way for me to make more money is to raise my prices, because I can't take on anybody else. But I'm already under contract with the people I have now, so I can't raise the prices on them because that's unethical and outside of our original agreement. What do I do?* I had to go back to the drawing board. I had to come up with a better idea, or I would find myself in a situation that wasn't as favorable as it had been in the beginning. So, that's what I did, went back to the drawing board.

Chapter 11: Salesman, CEO and Solo Employee

To recap: I was out of time; my business was taking off, and I was absolutely exhausted. At this point in my life, if you were to look back through my Facebook page, it's about 2015. You can tell that my hair's fried. I didn't really keep it cut that often because I was busy. I was working from 7:00 in the morning to 7:00 at night then spending time with my family and friends and the haircut place closed at 6:00. I didn't have a chance. You can see, I'm totally oxidized looking. If you scroll back through my social media channels and look at my videos, the exhaustion is plainly on my face.

I was going through real shit, and I realized when you're playing that video game of life, and you get to the boss at the end—I'll make that reference a lot in this book—they have weapons you've never seen before. You've prepared for a gunfight, and they've got nuclear weapons. You've prepared for a gunfight, and they've got fighter jets and tanks. It's not what you were expecting at all, and that's what happened to me.

At this point in my life, I'm salesman, CEO and solo employee. I'm running my own ads, making my own funnels, having my own sales conversations, running my own trainings. It is literally me. I'm chief bottle washer, cook and waiter all at the same time. And it's absolutely exhausting. It's wearing me out. I had to find a better way. So, I decided to step out of the salesman and solo employee role and into the CEO role more because to gain momentum in one area I had to let go of drag in other areas. The drag was me being a salesperson. The drag was me being the solo employee. When I let go of those drags, I could focus more on being the CEO.

Listen, my clients were demanding. They hit me up on the phone. They hit me up on text message. They hit me up with videos. They wanted me to look at their funnels. If you have 50 clients and they need an hour a week, that's 50 hours right there off the rip before you even get a second to yourself to bring on new clients. Using that ratio, my business was not scalable. I had demanding clients, business taking off, but I was beyond beat. I had to let go of the drag. I had to let go of being the solo employee and salesman and focus on being a CEO.

What does a CEO do? When you hire a CEO for your business, the CEO is the person who's supposed to optimize the profitability of your business. You see, I was so scared of being the CEO that twice in my career I had hired somebody else to be the CEO of my company. Both times, the person I'd brought on had failed. I identified as a salesperson, but I was about to take the leap from salesperson to CEO. To do so, I had to put on my CEO hat. It was no longer *how can we make sales today?* It was *how can we increase our bottom line and become a more profitable business entity?* I had to change my perspective, the way I looked at words, the way I conducted myself, the way I ran the company.

This change almost instantly evolved simply because of a different thought pattern and realization that took place. Let me tell you this, my friend, if you're in a situation where you're maxed out on your work, you're the salesman, the CEO, the solo entrepreneur, doing all the work yourself, you will find yourself maxing. The only way you can build an empire is with others.

You've got to learn to give up to get up. You've got to give up what holds you down to get to the next level. I needed to focus on being the CEO to gain momentum and let the drag of being a solo employee and salesman fall behind me. It wasn't easy for me because I identified as a salesman. But if I continued as a salesman I would only earn a salesman's wages.

The richest people in the world are not salespeople. Sure, they're undocumented salespeople, right? But the richest people in the world are CEOs. The richest people in the world are people who own businesses, not just salespeople. There are plenty of wealthy salespeople, but my plan in my life is to be one of the richest people in the world. If I'm going to do that I must make the shift to thinking and doing what the super, ultra, mega-rich do. They don't think like a salesman; they think like a CEO. If you're going to leverage your business, if you're going to be the most successful person in the history of your industry, if you're going to be the person growing an empire to make millions upon millions upon millions upon millions of dollars and leave a legacy, you need to think like a CEO and not a salesperson.

It was a dark moment for me because, like I said earlier, throughout my entire life, I've identified as a salesperson. I've always thought the CEO was the "man." It's 2017 as I write this book and I'm a full-fledged CEO. I've had to make the shift. As a salesman, I earned $250,000 to $500,000 a year. As a CEO, we do that in a month. My mindset adjustment, my focus, the things I'm about to share with you in the second half of this book will hopefully reframe your mind and open your eyes to what's possible, too. Here's the great news. Whether you're a sales guy inside of an organization or whether you are an entrepreneur who owns your own small business and you're reading this book, you are about to learn the shifts that will allow you to grow.

You can grow as a salesman within an organization. You can hire a team. If you look around, some of the most successful real estate agents work huge brands. They have teams. They've leveraged other people. Even though they might be a real estate agent, or they might be an insurance agent, or they might be a loan officer, they've started thinking like a CEO. They've said, "I am the CEO of my own sales business. How do I make my bottom line more profitable versus how do I go out and make more sales?"

Chapter 12: There's Gotta Be a Better Way

There's gotta be a better way, right? That's exactly what I sought out to find. I started thinking like a CEO. I said, "I've got a business with 50 clients paying me $2,500 a month, and I'm maxed out on time. I've got a seminar business where we can take 25 people on at $5,000 a pop, but I can't upsell any of those into my group, so I will run more events." And run events I did. Every month, when I put them on, it was exhausting because I was constantly selling, constantly filling and constantly delivering event material on top of already consulting 50 or so clients. It was only a matter of time before that model wasn't as profitable as I thought it would be, too. Again, if you think about it, I was running my head into the same problem I'd had before: lack of time.

Sure, I had Roxanne and Johnny working for me, and I'll talk more about the strategic hires that I made along the way in due time. Yes, the two of them were starting to make sales, starting to pick it up, but they had to go through their 90-day to six-month period to get there. Just because I had an epiphany in the middle of the night and a change in thinking, doesn't mean my team was fully-trained and ready to go. It doesn't mean the machine was armed. We still gotta make the bullets. We still gotta lace up our boots.

I put my thinking cap on to figure out new ways I could add to the bottom line. For example, I wasn't doing any affiliate marketing. I pushed a bunch of products onto the marketplace consistently, but I'd always let my ego and pride come before dollars. I would say, "I don't want to get an affiliate link from ClickFunnels or Leadpages or AWeber because I like the product and I'll endorse them regardless." But that's how a salesperson thinks. That's not how a CEO thinks. A CEO thinks *if they're offering free money, I should take it.*

I'm so glad I had that change of opinion because right now, I make about $10,000 a month on autopilot from affiliates and I have for years. That's $120,000 a year I was letting go. It's free money and a complete handout, yet I never took the opportunity to even open my palms. As the CEO, I saw affiliate marketing as a new opportunity to pay for my advertising budget. My advertising budget could sell digital products on autopilot, and then I wouldn't be stuck every single day delivering coaching sessions to actual clients.

I looked for sponsors for some of the events. I'd always paid for my own hotel. I'd paid for the room, and I had zero sponsors. As a CEO, I thought, *why wouldn't I get people I'm already doing business with to endorse us? Why wouldn't I take advantage of giving other people exposure, that will help their business?* So, that's exactly what I did, and as a result, we added another $25,000 a quarter to our income. In a short period of time, because of two quick decisions, I figured out how to add $250,000 a year to my bottom line. It all happened from a simple switch in my thinking from salesman to CEO. Again, even though the shift had occurred, my sales team still wasn't up to speed.

But suddenly I had recurring money from affiliates. I had people sponsoring my events. But guess what my stupid ass did? I just worked more. I threw more events. I tried to send out more affiliate marketing emails and focused on figuring out a shortcut. I had created a better way, but then I got in my own goddamn way, too. I wound up still dragging, slaving away in another inefficient system.

It was no different than when I was the solo employee. It was no different than when I was maxed out on clients. It was all the same. There I was, increasing my revenue while also increasing the amount of time I had to invest. I was tired to the bone. Oxidized, waking up early, working out, should've been in the greatest shape of my life, but just ass-worn-out from all the constant beatings of building funnels, marketing funnels, running ads, helping clients, closing clients, dealing with clients, selling this and that and solving problems.

It was never-ending.

I looked for ways to increase my revenue and every time I'd find a new place to pull money from: affiliate offers, sponsors for events, throwing events more often, whatever it was…none of those strategies allowed me to step away and let go of the drag, to let go of being the salesmen. None of those ideas allowed me to let go of being the only employee. I was taking off, and I had caught a massive amount of momentum, but I still chose to grab two big-ass heavy bags to bring along on the trip with me, even though I didn't need the shit inside.

Another month went by. Our revenue increased. I had no more energy and ultimately, no more money because I was spending it back on advertising and trying to grow. I was my own worst enemy because as I was trying to grow the business, I kept telling myself, *I'll just work harder* when I was already working as hard as fucking possible. When I truly couldn't take it anymore, I said, "Fuck it. I'm gonna do what I know needs to be done."

Chapter 13: My First Sales Team

Have you ever gone to get a haircut and the barber's hair looks like shit? Have you ever signed a deal with a real estate agent who lives in an apartment? Have you ever gone to a personal trainer who was out of shape? Have you ever been to a doctor who smokes cigarettes? As strange as these anomalies might sound, these weird relationships between people and their discrediting habits exist every single day in our society. These are people who are really, really, really good at something, but they abandon it, and I was no exception. I was really, really, really, really good at training people in how to make sales, but I had abandoned my sales team.

Sure, I had a few people working for me. Roxanne had no formal funnel sales skills. This wasn't her area. She knew how to sell a little bit, but she had been a housewife homeschooling kids for the last stint of her life. Sure, Johnny knew how to sell warranties and cars. That's the world he came from. But our business is completely different. My answer to salespeople who came on board was simple: "Listen to this audio and go to work." The audio was our CATCH training system, the five-step acronym we use to close people.

I was still exhausted out of my mind, maxed out on employees, while my sales team was confused as fuck and going broke.

Meanwhile, every day I asked the sales team, "Why the fuck aren't you guys making sales?" They were just too afraid to tell me, "Because you don't fucking train us!" I realized I had to make an example out of a salesperson and put all my faith and training into that person, and then I could either A) rely on that person to train others, or B) use that person as the shining example of what others want to be. So, one day, I taught Roxanne systems and the CATCH process. I taught her exactly what she needed to know to serve our business. After I trained her, the next thing I knew, she was making $15,000 to $20,000 a month on a consistent basis. At that moment, I knew I had done exactly what I had intended to do.

I started bragging about her in all our Facebook groups and on my posts. I started featuring her in some of our social media, talking her up to give credit where credit was due. This is an example of attraction marketing. I wanted to show people: "Look, this housewife who had been homeschool educating her kids is now going to make a quarter of a million dollars this year selling my product." Because of that, of course, the floodgates opened. Salesperson after salesperson sent me direct messages. They'd say, "Get me a job." At first, I wanted to help everybody, but as I said in a previous chapter, I realized many of them were getting our free sales training and then moving on to chase their own dreams.

Can you imagine how frustrating that's been? It almost feels sometimes like I've created my own competition. But then I got a system together. If somebody hit me up and said they were a badass salesperson, I would tell them I'm not hiring. If they said, "Okay, keep me in mind," then obviously they were *not* a badass salesperson. If they argued with me, tried to close me or handle my objections, I might just deal with them. At one point, I had so many people hit me up that we ran an *American Idol*-style hiring campaign. People gave us their sales pitches and tried to impress us with wacky stuff. I hired three people from the training. All of them sucked and all three got fired within a month.

I hired closer after closer. Now, you gotta remember, my reputation as a sales trainer was on the line with each of these people, and they had failed me miserably because I was focused on my clients who were paying me. I wasn't focused on the salespeople I felt would benefit the greatest from working for me for the simple fact that I had it all. I had leads; I had a system; I had everything in place for them to succeed. What more could these salespeople possibly want? They needed training, so lines and lines of closers assembled, and I hired and fired. When that happened, it soured my reputation in the marketplace. People developed the perception: "This guy doesn't keep people very long. He must be bipolar because he hires a person and then lets them go." The truth is I had no tolerance, and I wasn't a manager. I wasn't a CEO either even though I had been thrown into that role.

There are two types of leaders in this world: situational, and natural-born. I was not a natural-born manager; I was a situational manager. I was not a natural-born CEO; I was a situational CEO trying to hire people and manage them even though I had no experience. I left a lot of haters in my wake because new salespeople were so excited to come work for me, but then they didn't receive the training they'd anticipated. They had been turned over to the wolves, and that's why they failed. It probably caused more heartache for me than anybody else. Still, I knew I would make mistakes as I scaled to my full potential.

Chapter 14: I Always Feel Like Somebody's Watching Me

Everybody wanted to be on our team. While I don't look at myself as an authority or celebrity, I realize the marketplace does. They come work with us and realize I'm actually a cold, distant, go-do-it-yourself, no-shit-was-ever-handed-out-to-me type of person. It changes the perspective of the marketplace. You know, when you hire and fire 20 people in a short amount of time, that's 20 people that'll each tell 200 people.

In 2015, I hired a guy, and he got so mad when we fired him he said he was going to get on a plane, fly to Dallas and murder my entire family. I'm not the type to call the cops, so we waited it out to see if he would ever show up and we had a little surprise for him if he did. That's the kind of stress I had to deal with during this time of my life. This guy got fired for simply not making sales. But just as he'd talked shit about hurting my family, and then never showed up, he'd also talked shit about how he could close a lot of sales, but he didn't perform in either way.

Everybody wanted a piece of this job. They saw Roxanne and thought she had it so easy. Never mind, the six months she worked for me behind the scenes learning every element of the system.

Folks were trying to fools-rush-in on me, but what happened behind the scenes is no one wanted to do the work. We would give sales guys jobs and leads, and then the leads would fuck them up.

At the time of the writing of this book, I've owned three alarm companies, and I've fired two of them. I'm on my third alarm company. I hired doorknockers initially and gave them inbound leads. They were horrible and were so used to outbound prospecting that inbound leads fucked them up. The second time, I followed the same process because I hadn't yet figured out the inbound leads were the problem. I hired better doorknockers and thought the issues would clear up. But it was the inbound leads. The salespeople didn't know how to turn them into sales.

Even as it pertains to Hardcore Closer and Break Free Academy, if we give somebody too many leads it'll overwhelm them, and you can't talk to an inbound lead, in the same manner, you would prospect people. Our CATCH process should have solved all that, but you know how hardheaded salespeople can be.

"Oh, man, Stewman. Give me a bunch of leads. I'll close leads." I would dump 100 leads on somebody's lap, and they'd never call any of them.

Some of you are listening to and reading this book right now, and you're thinking, *how would somebody get 100 leads and not call them*? Congratulate yourself. You're wired differently than most people. The majority of people say they want to work, but their actions reveal a completely different intention.

Most people say they want to be a millionaire, but they have a minimum wage work ethic. Most people say they want to have a ripped six-pack and a large penis, but they're scared to go to the gym or take dick pills.

I've seen it. Hired a lot of closers who have failed. I've hired a lot of people who told me they were straight up savages who didn't know what to do with a lead when it arrived in their inbox. I always tell those guys, "Man, if you'd have tried to sell these leads as hard as you sold me on this job, you'd be making more money than me."

I had to learn how to deal with salespeople. It was one thing to have salespeople as clients. It was another thing to manage them. This was a big learning curve because I have no management skills and I know that *how you are is how you assume others are.* I'm a self-starter, and I assume everybody else is that way, too. Turns out most salespeople aren't. They need their hand held. They're delicate. They need their ego stroked.

But you don't get any of that here. That's not what we do at Hardcore Closer. We do the hard shit. We stay in our own lane. We put in the fucking work. But, man, it took me a lot of fucking effort to find out who the hell was willing to put in the work and who wasn't.

I went through a lot of bad salespeople and handed out a lot of leads until I came up with my own system on how to hire and fire.

Chapter 15: Cleaning House Weekly

Here I was, hiring and firing salespeople like it was something I loved doing. It was not because I don't like letting go of anybody. Let's be real. When you have to let go of somebody, they were expecting income, and you're cutting them off. You're telling them there's no way they can get their income with you. I've only been fired from one job in my entire life. It was a fucking terrible experience. I really feel like punching that smug fuck in his face just talking about it in this book. I had been generating quite a few loans for a mortgage company, and the CEO let me go. He said that I wasn't a good fit for the company, which meant I was making more money than they could afford to pay me. It fucked me up. I had to go home and face my then-wife and soon-to-be son knowing I'd lost my job.

Ultimately, it turned into a blessing because I started this business as a direct result. Still, I had to fire people, and I took no amusement in it. I actually had to put my game face on and go in there and tell people on the phone or through email or a message that: "Hey, you're not making sales. You're fired." It caused me to be callous, but then came the tipping point where I had hired and fired enough people and been through enough pain that a few folks stuck around.

The people who stayed with me started to get their job right. Roxanne stuck around. Johnny stuck around. Travis Plumb, who worked with me back in 2011, stuck around, too, and he started making sales. From there, we brought on another guy named Josh who made a few sales. Then we picked up a client named Ryan who also made a few sales.

I looked back at myself and said, "Holy shit! I get to fire myself. I get to fire myself from the sales position. I have hired and fired enough people and thinned the herd and cleaned the chaff enough to where I can finally fire myself from being a salesperson."

I could let go of those two big-ass heavy bags I talked about earlier, catch the momentum, release the drag and skyrocket the business.

The moment I fired myself, the business absolutely took off because I was no longer interfering in the sales. I was focused on the success of the clients and not the sales of the clients. Think about how that changed the game for them. The focus before had been making money and selling prospects into doing my programs. Then the focus changed to helping the prospects become more successful. Which do you think sounds better from a marketing perspective, "I like selling people products," or "I like helping people who buy from me to become successful"?

I wondered if I could fire myself from sales, in what other areas could I fire myself? Could I fire myself from managing the day-to-day operations? Could I fire myself from handling the books? Could I fire myself from doing all the paperwork? Could I fire myself from setting up the events? Could I fire myself from making the logistics of everything happen? What else could I fire myself from?

I made a list of shit I did every single day, of monthly chores and tasks that were demanded of me each year. I put a checkmark next to the ones I enjoyed doing. Those items included making content, writing books, writing blog posts, making videos, posting on social media, creating new outlets and new funnel schemes.

Then I realized all the tasks I didn't like doing: bookkeeping, paperwork, dealing with lawyers, managing the sales team, managing the office staff, putting in orders, setting up events. I just wanted to show up, create the content and change lives. That's all I wanted to do. Prior to that, I had to put in all the work myself, so I knew every single position in the company and how it should work. Yes, that knowledge allowed me to guide people better, but at the same time, I also wanted to fire myself from every single one of those positions.

When I worked at the car wash, I worked every position. From vacuuming cars to selling car washes to building the equipment, I had done it all. When a person came in, and they hit me with an objection, I knew everything about that car wash inside and out. I could close over it. I built Hardcore Closer the same way. I know every single position, including how all the websites were built. From the CEO's perspective, a lot of those areas were suffering because I was involved in them. I knew it was my time, that even though I had hired and fired a bunch of people, I now needed to hire and fire myself from numerous positions. I needed to hire myself into some other positions that greatly needed me as well. Any position hindering my momentum and causing drag had to go.

Chapter 16: Navy SEALs of Sales

After I'd let enough people go, I started letting myself go. Through that process, I discovered that decent people will self-govern themselves. You don't have to be a tyrannical boss or a militant leader. If you hire decent, loyal people and treat them right, they will govern themselves. They will decide their own hours they'll show up in the office. I've never told anybody a set number of hours to be in the office, or a set time, but they're here every day on time, on their time.

When I thinned that herd, and it started to govern itself, my man, Travis Plumb, who we had hired a few months before, stepped up in a big way. Within a year of his hire, he became top producer the second month out of the gate, and he has been there ever since. Before long, he was closing $300,000 months. That's right. He would make over $300,000 in sales in a month, but we had several other people making over $100,000 in sales a month as well. Roxanne and Josh have both exceeded that number many times.

While Travis has been the ultimate SEAL, I created a SEAL team of salespeople. These folks can sell via text message, via video, via blog post, via a phone call, face-to-face, from the stage, through email, FaceTime, Snapchat, Instagram, Facebook. You name it; they got it. They're SEAL, Sea, Air and Land. They cover it all.

When I looked up, we were mesmerizing the marketplace. People would say, "How did he build his company and where did he find those people?" That's when I realized great armies aren't built. They aren't found. They're trained. The reason why our military in American is the greatest military on the planet is because they do the work every single day. They wake up, routinely train, and they do it every single day. Wake up. Routinely train. Every single day. Even though I'm not a militaristic leader, I put those same rules into play at Hardcore Closer. Wake up, train, follow the regimen. The strong survived and all of a sudden, we had the best of the best.

Not a day goes by that one of my sales guys isn't offered a job somewhere else, but they shrug it off because they know better. They know there's no better job than this. Just like I had said all along, I created the ultimate sales job, Inbound leads, a known brand, an in-demand product, a follow-up system, a five-step phone audible conversation, a way to close via video, a way to close via text. I have set up my salespeople for ultimate success. All it took was me stepping out of my salesman role for a minute, and stepping into a sales trainer role, so I could be the person my team needed. The next time I looked up—during the time I was writing this book—we were close to doing seven figures in a month in one of our companies.

I made the investment in the time. I made the investment in my people. I made the time to impart my wisdom to my staff, and that investment has paid me back tenfold. There are over $14,000 in sales alone today as I write this. And I have no clue where they've come from. But they've all originated from the sales team. We're only halfway through the day right now. Our average sales day around here is somewhere between $20,000 and $30,000. It all comes from these Navy SEALs of sales: Travis, Ryan, Josh and Roxanne. It works because I've taken the time to be the barber with the good haircut, to be the website designer with the nice website, to be the doctor who doesn't smoke. In short: I invested the time and made the shit happen.

Now, I've got one of the strongest sales teams on the planet.

Chapter 17: Operation Nightmare

With this new growth taking over my company, I found I had a whole new problem. I've got bad-ass salespeople; I've let go of the drag, and I've caught momentum as the CEO. I was starting to get better at my decision making, but there was one problem. All this time I'd only had one person working as an admin. She was my original hire, the very first person to ever work for me. Actually, in the beginning, there were times Lindsay didn't get a paycheck, yet she still stayed on board. She believed in our vision that much. Now, I found her in the same position I'd been in six months to a year prior. She was beyond beat and had reached a critical mass to where the number of clients, requests and emails (and every other job on her plate) she was fielding on a daily basis caused her exhaustion and oxidation as well.

As a matter of fact, as I write this book, I'm proud of Lindsay because she's lost a lot of weight and taken back control of her health. As Lindsay was getting exhausted and juggling so much, I found out one more thing about myself that was a big problem. I have zero experience in hiring anybody other than salespeople. I've only worked with salespeople. I've only trained salespeople. I've only hired salespeople. I've only fired salespeople. I've only been hired as a salesperson. I've only been fired as a salesperson, and I know nothing about all the other operations that are supposed to be in an organization. All I know is Lindsay does it all.

I'm experienced enough to know at this point that it's not about finding another Lindsay. It's about recreating the experience for her. What is it that she's good at; what is it that she likes doing and what can we outsource that she doesn't like doing? We got to a point where it wasn't beneficial for her to continue working in the way she was, putting in the hours that she was. When she suggested that one of our clients and a good friend of mine named Patrick Grabbs, step into a role in our company I agreed.

Lindsay was helping me make the funnels and putting on the final touches and Patrick, who I'd known since 2011, had also come through a Break Free Academy and spent a lot of time at my house, hanging out, wanting to learn from me and wanting some mentorship. He ended up being the next hire. About six months before that, we had tried Patrick in a sales position, but it wasn't really what he wanted to do. He gets more fulfillment from the tech side of things. At the time, he expressed what he really wanted to do; there was no way I could afford to retain somebody else because I still had to train the sales team. Because of the turn of events in growth and our systems flowing smoothly, we could bring Pat onboard. He received additional training and improved in funnels, which relieved a lot of the pressure off Lindsay.

After about another three or four months, we brought in a guy named Tod Holland. Tod was a client, too. He'd gone through Break Free Academy Digital. He understood how to build funnels, and we hired him to help us with the funnel building process. Lindsay's job was cut in half because the majority of what she was doing was building things on the backend for us. I could see what we call the success team taking shape.

The success team's jobs are to make funnels and handle customer support. I added another level, as well, where when people sign up for one of our programs, they hop on an intake call with Mandi. She lets our clients know the benefits of membership and what their packages contain. She tells them what to expect and what they will get out of working with us.

These changes meant Lindsay did not have to call people and welcome them to the program anymore. Mandi handles that. She didn't have to create funnels, run any emails or marketing schemes because Pat handles that. Tod's running more of the funnels than Pat and Pat switched over to become our Infusionsoft guy who keeps our backend operational. We are building a machine to last, a machine that keeps running whether we show up at work or not. The leverage that we have as a team is way better than the leverage I had as an individual.

We had two divisions in our business at this stage in the journey, the success team, that consisted of Mandi, Pat, Tod and Lindsay and the sales team, with Roxanne, Travis, Josh, Ryan and Casey. Since the company was split into two divisions, we created a motto called Stay In Your Own Lane. The support team doesn't need to step over into the sales team's lane, and the sales team doesn't need to step over into the support team's lane. Our internal workings were rolling along just like I said would happen in a previous chapter. Folks were governing themselves, and beautiful turns-of-events were happening.

We transformed our operation nightmare into an empowering force, so we could ascend to the next level. We turned a weapon formed against us into a benefit for our momentum. All along, I had to deal with less and less shit as the CEO of the company, and that allowed me to spend more of my time and energy pushing company divisions further and further. As I put together sales and operations teams, my role as a CEO became clearer. The momentum we were catching doubled up. But just as I told you about in previous chapters, anytime momentum catches up to you, you better get ready because if you can't handle it, it will overwhelm you.

Chapter 18: Would the Real Closers Stand Up?

Overwhelming momentum brought some real closers. Some of them were artificial, and some of them were human. But as I demonstrated to the sales team, I was willing to invest in them to ensure they had better operations, to give them the right people to help them become successful in the backend, to make sure they had someone else supporting our clients instead of themselves. When I demonstrated I would support them in those ways, the momentum went on. They started making more sales. The real closers stood up. Travis had months where he hit between $300,000-$400,000 in sales. Roxanne would sell $100,000-$150,000. Josh would hit $80,000-$150,000. Ryan was closing two and three sales a day, too. It was game on over here.

I didn't have to talk to a single person they closed. Lindsay didn't have to talk to them either. Mandi onboarded them. Pat and Tod supported them. We had a synergistic system in place, and that caused massive momentum because people realized we were expanding and that we could help our clients in a bigger and better way than we had done before.

As a byproduct, obviously, the company became more profitable. The net bottom line swelled, and that allowed me to reinvest back into the business, so we could build a new, artificial intelligence sales team. This team was the perfect complement to our natural, intelligent sales team. We call our artificial sales team robots.

Patrick and Tod became so skilled at building funnels, and Pat was killing it working Infusionsoft. They put strategies in place that we call dynamic behavioral targeting. It's all based on how a person comes through our funnel, how they connect with and interact with us, on where they left the funnel in an email sequence and on their Chatbot sequence. Pat went to town building it all.

We had a system set up to sell Break Free Academy Digital, a $2,000 per sale product. Salespeople were selling Break Free Academy Live, a $5,000 per sale product, and they were selling The Tribe, a $25,000 per person product. They were selling these offerings left and right. The robots were tossing lay-ups to the sales guys. The robots coaxed the prospect to stick up their hand; then the sales guys reached out. We used a fire rating. When a prospect reached four flames, they were on fire, and it was time to call them.

Until then, we let the robots do their job. So, Pat built the robot empire, and the robots kicked in. For the first time ever, we had so many leads we had to get a CRM. One month, at one point in time, my Amex bill was $100,000 because our robots and our sales team were working so efficiently that we flooded their inboxes with leads and made them take every prospect they possibly could. With the sales team onboard, the real closers standing up, the robots closing deals, the CRM working, and the dynamic behavior response method implemented, we are absolutely, still to this day, crushing it. We are running on all fronts of our business.

When this happens, an influx of clients comes in, and again, I find myself at that same bottleneck. I have to go back to the admin staff. I have to expand our operations without exhausting people. That's the thing about business and being a CEO; it's a never-ending, delicate balance between operations and expansions. Every time a sale is made, that's more of a burden to your operations team, and you don't want a bottleneck anywhere in your business. One goal I learned from washing cars is that you want to have an efficient assembly line spitting out predictable results every single time.

That's what I ended up creating, and that's what I was working on at this point in my journey. The human closers were doing $500,000 a month. The robot closers were slowly catching up. Our advertisements ran directly to the robots, that made the sales and all pistons were firing. Just when we were at the top of our game from multiple perspectives, it was time to expand the operations department once again.

Chapter 19: Three Divisions

Ultimately, I hired a guy named Jose Escamilla, who was an old friend of mine. I hired a few other people to come in and help us out in variations, too. I hired an editor. I hired a guy named Matt Ganzak to run our ads. I hired Robert Wiesman to run our podcast and handle our media. As I'm going through the list of people, I realize I've got about 15 employees working for me. Maybe they're not all employees, but 15 people who are either independent contractors or employees have joined the team.

We had two divisions of the company working, but they were overlapping. Our motto, Stay In Your Own Lane was not working out that well.

One day, I was watching training from Ryan Deiss who is the CEO of a company in Texas called DigitalMarketer. He was talking about how his company was set up in three divisions. I thought, *well, that's really cool*, so I adopted my model around it. I like to sit here and take credit for the whole thing. We've done our own expansions, of course, but Deiss gave us the basis for it. I split my company into three divisions: the success division, the acquisition division, and the money division. I did this because our motto, Stay In Your Own Lane, was even more pertinent to each person. Since we've made that change, each team member has a clear description of their team and job functions.

The acquisition team's in charge of acquiring media, leads and technology that help us generate more leads. They're not in charge of sales. They're not in charge of anything other than acquiring leads. These guys make my funnels. They run the Facebook ads. They run the ads on YouTube. They do the creative work and make the media and the videos. They make the audios. They produce the podcast. These are the people who create all the lead gen material. The one and only job of the acquisition team is to acquire clients and prospects that we turn into clients. All day long, they focus on making funnels better, converting traffic at a lower cost, decreasing their cost per click, and optimizing other marketing elements in the background. That's their job: to acquire leads as cheaply as possible, but it's to also ensure they are as effective and scrubbed as possible.

The second division of my company is called the success team. Success means several things. If the guys on the acquisition team need help, the success team gives them a hand. If our clients need help or have questions, the success team is there. Every single week, Pat and Tod host a two-hour hangout for our clients and help them with their funnels and marketing. We call it Funnel Chat when Tod does it. It's Marketing Autopsy when Pat hosts. This team is focused on the success of our clients. That's all the success team does, set up everybody else around them for success, whether it be me, the sales team, the acquisition team, or our clients. Their job is to support and ensure everybody's successful in what it is they want. The success team creates the help. They advise on the ads. They create the content to help people with their funnels. They handle tech support. They manage all the jobs behind the scenes you never see, but they are dedicated to the success of our entire team, and that includes our clients.

The third division is the money team. The money team is in charge of one thing and one thing only: sales. The acquisition team sends them leads. The success team makes sure everything is handled on the backend once they make a sale. My money team only focuses on sales. They get a lead. They call a lead. They close the lead. They collect the money and turn it over to the success team. If they don't close the lead, they keep following up until they do. They have one job: to get money. That's why we call them the money team. It's the dream job that I wish I would've had when I was a sales guy. I created it for them. I've created the support staff around them as well because I know that any good company is sales-driven. Those are the elements that make us money. As long as my acquisition team's generating leads and my sales team is making sales, I'll always be able to afford the salaries of the success team. A lot of companies get it backward. They obsess over optimizing costs per clicks and all the other strategies so hard that they miss out on the people who truly drive their business: the money team. My money team is the Navy SEALs of money teams.

At that point, we had three divisions: acquisitions, success, and money and our motto: Stay In Your Own Lane. Since we know to stay in our lane, what happens is the folks govern themselves again, and they don't cross over the lines, but instead, they ask people on the other side of the lines to engage help. It was pretty amazing to see that once everybody was clear 100 percent on what their title was, they were also clear on everybody else's title and responsibilities. Some awesome magic came into play. To this day, we run three divisions. That's all we need. Every time we add somebody, we let them know what team they're on. Every time we're in a Wednesday company meeting, we check with the teams because those three divisions are how we govern this entire business. I thought the motto we had established was clear, but I would soon find out, we had a little veer in my teams' mindsets. I needed to clarify my expectations even more.

Chapter 20: Stay In Your Own Lane

Now that we had three divisions I needed to make it absolutely clear who was responsible for what. In the past, I'd never really had a managerial job. It's never been a desire. I've always identified as a salesperson, and I knew in the sales world that when you did a good job, the bosses would come to you and ask if you wanted to move into management. Everybody I knew who was in sales management was not making as much money as they had been when they were in sales. They were miserable because their paycheck was totally reliant on the backs of other workers, and they always complained about the one thing that everybody in any kind of management complains about: employee drama.

Well, I started experiencing some of that employee drama myself. The sales team would get mad at the acquisition team and then suddenly; the sales team would try to generate leads. Then the acquisition team would try to generate sales. Hell, at one point, even my administrative staff, the operations division, attempted to close sales. We had three divisions, three tasks, but I wasn't sure who I wanted to do what at that point. That's when it hit me.

We had to embrace our company motto. It was easy to understand and should have been simple to apply. So, I brought it up again: Stay In Your Own Lane, and this time I made it stick.

How could the operations staff operate at peak performance if they detoured into making sales? How could the sales team close at peak performance if they derailed into handling operations stuff? My sales team should close sales and collect money; they shouldn't focus on helping people with support or look at people's funnels, or provide tech support to clients. Their job, 100 percent, is to make sales and if one of our clients had a tech support issue, it wasn't their job to support the client. Their job was and is to close prospects.

The same concept applies to the rest of the teams, but we had problems regardless. The administrative team and the operations team would post in our sales chat group that they had closed a sale. When that happened, the sales team came after me, saying, "Why are you letting them steal our leads and allowing the Harolds to close?" Every day, brought new drama until I reinforced Stay In Your Own Lane. It sounds easy enough when you say it, but to stay in your own lane, you must have people in their lanes. Since I have three divisions, we'll just say that I had three lanes. I learned I had to be crystal clear about who was to stay in what lane and who was not to cross over the other line.

Obviously, everybody on my sales team was instructed to stay in their lane. The money team was instructed to stay in the money lane. The success team was taught to stay on the path of supporting clients, supporting the salespeople, and not jumping to the front lines but to stay behind the scenes. Here's what behind the scenes means. It means supporting clients, giving them log-ins, giving them info, fighting refunds and processing paperwork with our merchants. It also means supporting clients with their log-ins and supporting clients by investigating their funnels. It means supporting clients by answering their questions, as well as engaging with them through the comments we post in our mastermind group, and so forth.

The acquisition team's job is to secure leads only. If the sales team is not closing leads, it is not their job to step up and start closing leads. Their job is to stay in their own lane and generate leads. If the sales team is not closing leads, they're supposed to bring that issue to me, which allows me to have the conversation with the sales team. I can say "What's going on? We've got the leads, what's the deal with the closing?" Now that I have this newfound way of looking at everything, I've led everybody into their own path.

"You, you're in sales, you stay in the money lane." "You, in success, you stay in the success lane." "You're in acquisition; you stay in the acquisition lane and please do not cross over because every time you cross over that means you're out of your lane." If you cross over between lanes in real life you could get pulled over for a DWI: Driving While being an Idiot. I would encourage you in your business to look at how you can divide two, three, four lanes, or however many lanes you need to benefit your business. You could segment your business into specific lanes and from there ask how you can assign your people to stay in those lanes.

As a CEO and a leader, as a person who's built up a business from the sales side to where we are now, I have a bigger vision than everybody else. I understand how to do every job. I can close sales, make funnels and run the operations, I just simply choose not to. I select people who are better than me to step up to each of those positions. Instead of being mediocre in these positions, I choose to put experts into each and every one of those lanes.

To get the most out of the experts, they have to have a clear set of expectations and a clear set of rules. Keeping them in their own lane and explaining their job to them, so they understood their expectations changed the game for me. I no longer hear people complaining that operations are closing their sales. I no longer have to deal with people complaining that sales aren't closing sales because they're out generating leads. We have a well-oiled machine.

Guess what? When your team members know their responsibilities, and they know every other team member's responsibilities, there's no guesswork. There's no *should I do this job*? Because they have clarity, and clarity brings focus, which encourages your momentum. That's what happens when you set up lanes for people, and you teach them to stay in their own lanes.

Chapter 21: Tipping Point

The crew was staying in their own lane. The machine was running on all cylinders. I realized that to catch momentum and pass the tipping point and rocket into the sky, you've got to let go of the drag. Some of the drag came from our team not paying attention, not focusing on why the leads were this way or why the leads were that way, or why the sales team wasn't doing this or why the support team wasn't there.

The situation caused a massive tipping point. Our program, Break Free Academy Live typically runs between $5,000-$8,000 for an event, and I was selling five or 10 people into each event if I was lucky. Then I put the sales team in charge, and we were not missing leads. I was playing follow up instead of catch up. I was leading. Suddenly, we started seeing 25, 35, 45 people attending every Break Free Academy. We were getting bigger and bigger.

Still, I had problems.

The first challenge was that I threw Break Free Academy in my penthouse building. I lived in an apartment, and it was pretty fly with the elevator that opened right up into my place. I had no front door, but I did have my own door guy, one of the greatest experiences of my life. On the fifth floor of that beautiful building, which I dearly miss now that I'm thinking about it, was the Aqua Lounge. It was a comfortable space with some TVs, furniture and a pool. Quite a posh spot to entertain people and have birthday parties or whatever other bash you wanted to throw. It was completely open to the residents, but you could also reserve it, so that's where we had our Break Free Academy.

Once, in late 2015, we were hosting our Break Free Academy Reunion, an annual meetup that we do every year. There weren't enough Wi-Fi spots for people to log in. We had about 40 people, and there weren't enough chairs either. It was the most frustrating Break Free Academy to date. Two people almost broke their computers because they were so aggravated. When you're dealing with tech issues, that happens sometimes, especially with Alpha personality types. Sadly, I knew I had grown out of the space. After two years, I had gotten too big for the Aqua Lounge.

To solve this problem, we started throwing Break Free Academy events at hotels. Making that change gave us some semblance of legitimacy because people went from, "This dude does it in his house," to "This dude's the real deal," when 50 people showed up. At the next one, we had 60 guests, but there were big problems that came along with booking one of the hotels. I had to learn a seriously hard lesson.

To prepare for the event, we would do a room block. But once we couldn't fill up the room block, and the hotel made me pay for the rest of the rooms. That ran me about $20,000 in rooms. It cost me more to pay for the rooms than it did for me to throw the event. I was so damn mad at the hotel because had I known they were going to charge me for the rooms and keep them those nights, I would have let homeless people sleep in them. I would have called my friends and told them they could take their significant others on a date. I would have entertained. I would have given those rooms away. Had I known I was going to pay for them, I would have used them.

We ran into one problem after another, and then I joined the country club. There happens to be one in the neighborhood, close to my home I just moved into this past year. To recap: I left the apartment, moved to a home, joined the ClubCorp and started throwing our events at the country club. It was only a matter of time before we outgrew that space, too. Once you get to about 60 people, most country clubs aren't accommodating. At least, not for all-day sessions that include Wi-Fi and every other amenity.

As I write this book, I'm in an office in North Dallas, and we have a conference room that holds 75 people, but the problem is we usually sell 90 tickets. We're going to have these events more frequently, but we've hit another huge tipping point. We've had about 1,000 people go through our programs, enough to make a significant impact to where others want to get involved. The results are there. The classes continue to get better. I just wrapped up my 23rd Break Free Academy Live last week. After hosting quite a few of them, we've gotten tremendous results.

The reason we are successful is in part due to Marshall Sylver. He was speaking at one of his Turning Point seminars, and he invited me to come out and take a look at how he ran his business. I immediately caught on to what he was doing. He's brilliant. I came back and deployed some of his strategies I learned at Turning Point to an audience of 75 people at my Break Free Academy seminar. When I did that, our events went from $3,000-$8,000 per ticket to a sudden and massive amount of upsells. At our last event, we made over $600,000 in just one weekend.

Now, obviously it takes years in the making to build this type of revenue and follow-up, but because of the team I've built, because of the support we have, because of the track record of helping our clients get the results they want, we're handling business. We're growing, and people want to be a part of it. Our program called The Tribe, the upsell of our Break Free Academy, is $30,000 a year at the time of this writing. It's the only program that allows people to consult and train with me personally. I'm not really a coach; I'm more of a consultant and trainer. But a membership in The Tribe is the only way you will get personal interaction with me.

In early 2017, we had an influx of Tribe people. Right now, The Tribe has over 100 members, which is about as many people as I can handle by myself. I am aiming to scale and build a couple different initiatives with two members of The Tribe; they're going to be the coaches and trainers, who allow no excuses. It will be absolutely amazing to see what we do from here.

When you hit a tipping point, when you catch momentum, the last thing you want to do is get dragged down by a draft. Each time I've run into one of these obstacles, I make adjustments to keep the momentum and let go of the drag. The drag, in this case, happened to be my beautiful apartment that I loved. The drag happened to be the country club where I had a blast throwing events, the club where I'm still a member. The drag happened to be the awesome hotels where we drank and had a good time. It was all super convenient, but those days are gone.

The tipping point can be where you take off, or it can be the point where you go from going up to going down. The last thing that I want to do is go down or face drag, so I'm riding the tipping point out. But, it's exhausting. Just holding the live events, doing the consulting and training, it still consumes my hours.

Although my team was supporting people, and the sales guys were making sales, I was still the only person at this point in my story, who could deliver the training and the consulting. Something had to give because I needed to add more hours back into my life. Once again, I found myself in the middle of a conundrum.

Chapter 22: The Entourage

In November 2016, I got an email from Frank Kern, one of the first mentors I ever hired. Frank extended an opportunity to me to spend two days with him at his house in a fancy pants part of California that I'd never been to before. I took him up on the offer, paid the amount of money that was required for me to make the trip, booked my flight and the hotel and took off to meet Frank. When I arrived at his house, it was nothing short of stunning. An armed guard sat at the front gate, and you had to pass through two more gates before you could get to Frank's huge house resembling the hotel from the movie *The Shining*. I mean it was just amazingly large, and I asked Frank, "Hey man, what do you need all those fences for?"

He said, "I don't know who *they* are, but they're definitely out there, and they're not getting in here." I always thought that was hilarious. Classic Frank paranoia. I sat down with Frank not knowing what to expect. "I know I'm in a rut. I'm stuck. I'm in a jam, and I've got to buy my time back." Well, Frank looked at my current business model, and we talked about possibilities for this, that and the other. He asked me about recurring revenue, and I explained I didn't have any. Everything we were doing was a one-off product sell, and the recurring monthly income was something that we'd just never implemented. He said, "You're missing out on a big chunk of business that's easier to handle. It's better, and it's leverageable." What he said answered a lot of the questions I had and solved a lot of the problems that had come along with those questions.

We created a program right there at his house called Break Free Academy Entourage. I finalized and launched it about a month later. Break Free Academy Entourage became the digital version of Break Free Academy. We sold the program for $1,997, and people would get a log-in. That was it. We had one shot to sell a person on it and then we would have to sell them something else like a membership into our affiliate program.

The Entourage program was a recurring monthly payment model, for $297 a month, but it gave you access to Break Free Academy Digital unlimited as if you'd paid the two grand for it. As soon as a person stopped paying, their access was denied. On top of that, we decided to send people monthly gifts. They received presents in the mail like a newsletter and maybe a keychain, a cool looking membership card or a USB flash drive. We sent a different piece of swag every month that was attainable, touchable and consumable, so the clients felt like they were getting more for their money than just the digital training that was uploaded and updated three times a week.

I'll never forget what Frank said to me right before I left his house and went home to launch the program. "This program means you won't have to wake up in the morning and wonder where your next paycheck's coming from. You'll know exactly how much you're going to make for the month, especially if you can account for attrition." Then he got serious. "You're going to go through some things that will be really heavy and really hard called the fish hook."

I didn't know what he meant at the time, and I'll explain the fish hook in the next chapter. When I learned about the fish hook, I had no idea how difficult times were going to get. His words have resonated with me so much that I set aside an entire chapter to explain the fish hook and what I personally went through when I figured out just what the fuck he meant.

Chapter 23: The Fish Hook

Have you ever looked at a fish hook? I like to fish. In my neighborhood, we have a couple of big ponds with huge catfish and bass. My neighborhood has golf courses and country clubs and inside those golf courses and country clubs, are tons of wildlife. There are lots of rabbits and squirrels, but in the ponds, there are also huge fish. So, like any true redneck, even though it says no fishing everywhere you look on the land, I went to Walmart and bought a fishing pole, some hooks and lures and caught an eight-pound bass out of that lake, mind you, ladies and gentlemen. So, I think I've still got it.

If you notice at the end of the fish hook, there's a little barb that starts low and then goes high real quick. It's short, too. It hits the peak, right at the tip of the hook and then slides down the tip to the bottom of the hook. There's a huge tip, and then a quick barb. The quick barb hops up a couple of millimeters before the fish hook goes down maybe a half inch. The middle of the fish hook is at the very, very bottom and once you make it through the bottom of the fish hook, the other side is long.

That analogy is a good example of how business works, and especially when you're just getting an idea or business off the ground. Frank Kern warned me that we would be headed for a fish hook. He said, "Ryan, you're going to go through what I call the fish hook." Instead of trying to reinvent the wheel and call it something else, I'll just use Frank's wording.

We launched the program December 15, 2016, and immediately, upon release, 50 people signed up. Within our first month, 100 people had signed into our program which was awesome. The program is still available to you. It's $297 a month. Just go to BreakFreeAcademy.com/ Entourage. You will get all the training and all the materials I talked about.

Here comes the fish hook. We had stopped selling our bread and butter maker, Break Free Academy Digital that we had used to push people into the continuity program. Well, in order to keep my sales team from not leaving me and starving to death, I had to give them commissions upfront because 300 bucks for a monthly membership is not very much money. To keep the operations team afloat, I had to invest a whole lot of money. To pay my personal bills and the office and all the other expenses, I had to invest a lot of money. When February rolled around, we had only made $50,000 from the program. That may sound like a lot, but we were used to making $200,000-$300,000 a month. Just like that, we were cut off.

When the dust settled, all we had left was The Tribe and the live event. The last one had been in September, and the next live event wouldn't take place until January. We were barely scraping by because of all the bills. The second month after that, it was the same situation. Then we had ad spend to account for, too. We had the price of technology, commissions upfront, operations costs, it all hit me. Every dollar I had saved up, I had spent by March. I had squirreled away money for years and by March was out of it.

My friend Jay Kinder once told me, "Your ability to become successful is in direct proportion to your ability to withstand financial pain." So, I withstood the pain, and there were times when I'd call Patrick, my VP and I'd be like, "Pull the plug. Let's go back to selling digital." And he'd say, "We've got to stay the course, man." The next week he would call me and say, "Pull the plug. We've got to fucking make some money, man." I'd say, "We've got to stay the course." We stayed the course. In April, we finally broke even. May, we saw a little profit. Not in the sense of breaking free from the previous months, simply from the perspective of paying that month's expenses. We were still behind for March, February and January.

That profit was enough to pay for the first three months' losses. By the time June came around, I had an extra couple hundred thousand dollars back in the bank account. By July, the number doubled. In August, the number quadrupled and I knew we had survived the fish hook Frank Kern had warned would get us! Thank God, he had given me a heads up! Surviving that fish hook kept us on course and brought us to the point where we have built up million-dollar months as a recurring revenue model.

Now, I want to talk to you about the fish hooks that you go through. See, most business owners, who start small businesses, end up quitting. They get deep in that fish hook. The bottom for us was March. I was out of money. The commissions had been paid upfront. I was spending money on ads. I was losing my ass. I'm having to ice my butt hole, right? But I stayed with it. Most people tap out, and I wanted to tap out, but I had an accountability partner, Patrick, who kept me in check. Patrick wanted to tap out sometimes, too, but he had an accountability partner: me. When he wanted out, I kept us in and vice versa.

Most business owners just quit. They say, "We can't go another month." The truth is we *couldn't* go another month. I was whipping out credit cards. Early on, when I started the business, I had opened a bunch of credit cards that I hardly ever use. But over the years, credit lines have been extended to me. I was offered zero percent financing on balance transfers and other incentives, so I've got seven credit cards I could use at any time with huge-ass lines. I thought I was going to have to break out one of the credit cards. But we stayed the course that month, and now it's paying off.

Right now, the program is doing $250,000 in sales every single month, and the monthly revenue that's coming from it is snowballing fast.

This is the challenge I want to issue to you. As you make the transition from salesperson to CEO and start your own business, things are going to go really well and take off quickly in the beginning. Those first 50 people were easy. Those next 100 people were a snap, but the break-even was 500 people. That barb, it starts low and goes high quick. The rise is just a couple of millimeters, but it's a long dip down to the bottom of the fish hook before you turn it around.

Most people quit at the bottom of the fish hook. You might be going through the fish hook right now, and you'll find you can't go back or you'll get stuck by the barb. You've got no choice but to keep going forward. Trust me, once you make it through the pain and once you make it through the other side, the pleasure is oh, so sweet and worth it.

Chapter 24: Attrition Fighters

One thing nobody told me about or warned me about was attrition. When I sold multilevel marketing, I knew attrition was a real concern, but most multilevel marketing products are overpriced and full of shit, so I never thought about attrition in my business with Break Free Academy Digital. We basically had a nonexistent refund ratio. Nobody ever asked us for their money back. We had 100 percent satisfaction from our customers. It was a great business. Nobody asked for their money back from the live events. Nobody asked for their money back after joining our Tribe for $30,000. So, attrition was something I had never faced.

To fill up the Break Free Academy Entourage program, I wrote a book called *Elevator to the Top*. If you'd like a copy, you can get one for free at ElevatortotheTop.com while supplies last.

In *Elevator*, I took my top 40 blog posts, arranged them in order and then had my editor turn them into a book. This book contains everything you need to know about business, from day one to retirement, and we give it away for free. This is how it works: you go to the site and get the book, then you have to pay a $7.00 shipping fee. From the $7.00 shipping fee, we can tell if you're a human, which we do want to verify before we start mailing books out all over the damn place. It costs us postage, paperwork and paying the fulfillment company, so readers paying the $7.00 is totally reasonable. After people buy the book, they get an opportunity to join Entourage, and if they don't join Entourage, they get an opportunity to watch a webinar that tries to sell them on Entourage. That's how our funnel works.

I was used to dealing with people who were paying $2,000, $5,000, $8,000 and $30,000. A person who pays $7.00 for shipping versus one who shells out $297 in recurring monthly income is a different kind of person. Now I love everybody, and I'm here to help everybody, but this lower price point attracted a lot of people who would get mad and say we stole $7.00 from them. Or, they would fume and say they hadn't given permission to charge their card.

Attrition took hold. People were dropping off and requesting refunds. I had never experienced it ever before. But I had never sold a lower-tier, lower-cost product. It was a whole new world for me.

The average attrition rate in our market was 27 percent. That meant out of every 100 people we added, 27 of them would drop off. 27 x $297 is a significant amount of money. Yes, you know every month you're adding 100 people, but really, you're only adding 73 new clients. We had to figure out a way to make it better. We were not going to plan on losing a third of our people every single month. A) We had a no-man-down policy. B) Our shit's better than the average industry, so we had to step it up and figure out how to solve this new problem.

Well, one of the problems was the Entourage. We were giving people 100 percent access to all of Break Free Academy Digital, which contained about 110 videos and audios. It was overwhelming. Let's say you join a program for two grand and you get 110 audios. You're like, "Okay, cool. I own this for forever." But if you jump into a recurring model, and you see that there are 110 videos, you can't think about consuming them all. People might say, "Man this is like something that's never going to go away." It's intimidating, like drinking from a fire hose. If you're trying to get your money back in month one, where do you start? The structure led to a lot of confusion, frustration and anxiety for our members. That's why we whittled down from 110 videos to eight videos.

After we made the change, when people logged in, they would see they had eight videos waiting. This simplified the program. It took our attrition from 22 percent to 12 percent. The industry standard again is 27 percent. We saved 10 more salespeople or 10 more marketers or funnel closers every single time. Every single month.

We were only losing 12 percent for every 100 who signed up. And that was 10 more we were saving, almost 20 people less than the industry average. We started thinking, *okay, so we're sending the monthly gifts. We are doing training twice a month. What else can we do for our clients?*

We added something called Funnel Chat with Tod, where he builds funnels once a week with our Tribe members. People don't get to interact with him, but they do see him work.

Clients also get something called a Marketing Autopsy where they can submit a form so my man, Patrick will look at their funnel and marketing and correct it. This helps them out, tells them how they should run ads and shares other tactics with them to ensure they improve their results.

Everything we are doing creates a queue of people who are interested in having their funnels looked at, so they're willing to wait, which is awesome. They feel like they get help, and then there's also fewer materials, but more strategic content, so they won't feel overwhelmed. Lastly, I make sure that my team comments on every single post in our Facebook group every single day. These are paying members, and it is highly important I make sure that every single day, their posts do not go unnoticed. Interacting with them lets them know we give a shit about them, that we're happy they're there, and we love to help. Because of that, we became attrition fighters, and have lowered our attrition rate significantly. When someone quits, it's shocking now. It's not like, "Oh no, again?"

Oftentimes, when someone's credit card doesn't process, or there is another technical issue, we find out that person wasn't necessarily quitting. In those instances, we just call them and get another card. This is the law of numbers, and you will notice it in play more often, especially, as your client count rises.

Chapter 25: The Path to 1,000 Clients

In each previous chapter of this book, we've put together the play-by-play to build what I would consider the perfect company for our industry, especially since we've pretty much created our own industry. We have the right team in place, the right corporate structure. We've fought attrition, so now the path is to start adding as many people as possible.

When I talked about the fish hook a few chapters ago, I mentioned that in June we'd made it out of the fish hook and started showing a profit for the first time. Part of that was reducing the attrition, and the other part was acquiring 100 clients a week.

We know for every 100 clients we get, 10 to 14 are going to leave. That means if you have 1,000 clients 140 are leaving. We set a clear path in December to hit 1,000 clients, and by August we had done it, except we weren't fortunate enough to retain them all yet. At the time of the writing of this book, we have a little over 600 active clients, but we do not have 1,000 active. However, we have had over 1,000 people come through the program, and I'd like to share with you how we got to those first 1,000 clients in the Break Free Academy Entourage Program.

The first action we took was to set a clear goal. In December 2016, I sat down and identified a goal and a plan to reach that goal for myself and my team. We aimed to have 1,000 clients by December of 2017—which we've obviously passed up earlier this year—and to not only have 1,000 clients by 2017, but, to move into an office, to scale the business, take it to the next level, and to meet some of the other goals I had outlined in our goal sheet. I'm talking internal, corporate, targets. We've been attacking these goals one at a time.

A lot of people will set annual goals, and they'll say, "Let's try to make all these goals happen at once." I'm smart enough to know that you can't get a bunch of projects done at one time. It drives me nuts when I go out to one of the houses we're flipping, and I see the general contractors have ripped the sheetrock off the wall, gotten half the fricking plumbing pulled out, half the electrical is gone, some of the roof is done and a chunk of the backyard's finished.

I'm like, "Why not finish one thing before you start another?" But that's how most people are. They have entrepreneurial ADD, and it doesn't have to necessarily even be entrepreneurial. It can just be ADD. They get something started; it gets boring. They move on and begin something else; that gets boring. So, they keep going and start something else. I'll be damned if they ever finish what they've started. That's what closers do. We finish things. That's a CEO's job—to make sure people finish what they start because, without a finished, completed project, there's no profitability.

We had to start picking off these goals one by one. We knew that we had an entire year before we needed to hit 1,000 people in our program, so the first goal we set our sights on was getting the fuck out of the fish hook. Once we'd accomplished that, the second goal was getting into an office, where we could collaborate. We had reached a tipping point; it no longer worked for us to conduct business as a remote team with everybody stationed at their homes. It made a lot more sense for us to be in one central location.

Everybody's moved to Dallas, where there are no state taxes and the cost of living is totally affordable. The part of Dallas that we live in offers anything you could want across the country, other than the beach and snow. Those are the only two things you have to leave the state to experience. Anything else you could want, any store, any food chain, any anything you could possibly want, it's right here in this area. It's not all boots, horses, carriages and cowboy hats like the TV and the media would have you believe.

We're attacking these goals. In April, we signed the lease on the new office in Dallas. By July, we had moved in. I'm writing this entire book, from our new corporate headquarters in Addison, Texas. It's 3,400 square feet, and way nicer than I envisioned it would be when we first decided we needed an office. We have a nice common area that holds 75 people that we consistently max out for Break Free Academy.

Now that we've set our goals, we obviously track them by checking them off. Our dashboard tells us how many people are members of Break Free Academy, how many have become members in the last week and month, and how many people have dropped out. It's a real-time look at people and statistics. As people drop out of our programs, our sales team calls them and asks them why they left. They do their damnedest, to get them right back on board with us.

I have to admit while it's one thing for me and my VP to set goals, it's another to get the entire corporation to understand the vision, and align themselves with those goals, to make our goals their goals. That's a completely different, game-changing situation. So, we began having phone call meetings every single day of the week at 9:00 AM. The meetings are usually 5 to 11 minutes, but at 9:00 AM everybody logs into a conference call, and I go over the goal for the day. Now that we're in the office, we don't do the phone calls. We have office meetings once a week for two hours. My general manager has accountability meetings every day with people for 5 to 11 minutes, and now I only run the weekly meeting, that educates everybody on what's missing, where we can improve and that reinforces our processes and systems.

Our processes are always improving. If I find a better way to make sales, you're damn right I'm going to share it with my team. Nothing is stuck in stone here. If they find a better way to make sales, then they'd damn sure better share it with the team and me, too. Now, we run these team meetings like sales trainings. I do three trainings. One for the sales department, and one for the success team. I do a training for the acquisition team during the two hours we run our meeting once a week.

However, I do that training in front of all our people, so that each person sees what the other people have on their plate. Doing things this way creates a newfound respect, and ensures all our goals are congruent. I'm telling you, once you get your team's goals in unison and to respect the hustle of each other, (because in a lot of corporations and a lot of settings people look at each other and say, "Well, this motherfucker's not working as hard as me," or, "This person gets paid more than I do, and they don't do as much work"), it absolutely alters and improves every aspect of your business.

We don't have any fucking complaining because everyone stays in their own lane. They trust that I've made the best financial decisions for the position they're in, and they respect what each person on the team is doing because nobody in my company is lazy. Lazy people don't work here. No underachievers work here. When the money team sees that the success team's working hard and the acquisition team's working hard, it makes them want to work hard. That's how we run our meetings as well, with full transparency and accountability, so that everybody knows what they're expected to do and how to stay in their own lane as they follow through.

Chapter 26: Total Accountability

Let's talk about aligning goals with your team members and keeping their goals in check, how meetings should work and what total accountability means. You see, if you're going to get the most from a human being, they have to be held accountable. And it's not because people can be lazy. It's not because people are deceitful or that they don't want to work hard. It's simply that people forget. We're busy. Lots of things jockey for our attention on a daily basis. Lots of people out there would like to distract us. Lots of outlets exist that draw our attention. We think we'll have made 100 phone calls when really, we've only made 20. But sometimes, those 20 phone calls feel like 100, and then we convince ourselves that we've made 100 when that's not actually the case. Without any accountability, the other 80 calls won't get made.

You must have total accountability if you're going to run a company, period. You need to know every person's job, what's expected of them and what is the best way for them to go about doing that job. We conduct daily accountability meetings the first thing in the morning. I have run these meetings forever. My general manager runs them now. They're five to 11 minutes, and it's, "Here's what happened yesterday. Here's what's going on today. And here's what's got to be done by the end of the week." That is the basis of the meeting.

This is the format we follow. First, we give somebody big ups. "Hey, congratulations to Pat for capturing a bunch of leads yesterday." "Congratulations to Arielle for making a ton of sales yesterday." We always lift somebody up first. We want to get the good shit out of the way and get them in a positive mood. We want them to show up on time for that meeting anticipating the first thing they might hear is the announcement of something cool they did.

After the acknowledgments of achievements, we let them know what happened the day before. It's good news or bad news or in-between. *Hey, here's where we were at yesterday. It's not so good.* Then we talk to them about what needs to be done today. Today our goals are x, and this is what we expect to happen. Then we'll talk about what's due long-term. Usually, for us, it's the end of the week. *By the end of the week, I expect to have 100 sales,* and so on and so forth. We do this to establish daily accountability, so everybody knows where we're at, what we need to do, and the goal. You can ask anybody at my company at any time what the goal is for the company and they know. They won't make a broad statement like, "To make more money," or "To get more customers." They will say, "The goal is 1,000 paying customers by the end of the year." One of the managers or I will say, "What's the goal of the Hardcore Closers?" "The goal is 200 paying Tribe members by the end of the year."

They know the goal, and they're focused on it. "What are you going to do to get there?" "We're running Facebook ads, and we're acquiring leads at a 30 percent option rate, and closing them at 20 percent of that. We're repeating that process over and over, scaling and hiring until we achieve this by December." It's really simple. Everybody knows the path here because we hold daily meetings in a format that's informative. Now, we also do a weekly meeting that's two hours every Wednesday from 10:00 to noon. Everybody meets in our main room, in front of a whiteboard. The first thing I do is talk about where we're at since we met last. I ask people if they need to address any points, and so early in the meeting, they address the things that matter. As they do, I write them down on the whiteboard. After I've written down everybody's contribution, I go back and address the issues that were on the whiteboard.

Once that discussion is over, I hold trainings that might be about how to follow up as a sales team. Maybe how to acquire a lead for the acquisition team. Maybe how to support people, or how to make sure there are no posts that don't have comments inside our networking and Facebook groups. I do these trainings every week. Sometimes it takes an hour. Most times it takes two hours, but I get everybody on the same page. Everybody knows the common goal, and everybody knows what the other person's doing to achieve that common goal. When we are all in alignment like this, it creates something called ecstasis. The book *Stealing Fire*, explains the concept of doing a bunch of psychedelic drugs and linking up to people. The Navy SEALs believe in ecstasis, too. I don't know if they use that word or not, but they operate on an ecstatis connection with other team members when they're out in the field or going through practice.

I practice ecstasis, too. I'm not giving my employees psychedelic drugs or Navy SEAL training over here, but we're all synced up in the same way. If Pat's making a funnel one way, then Lindsay's completing what she needs to on the backend to tie it all together. They don't have to communicate because they're both synced up to what their job is and the role they play.

It hasn't always been this way, and I'm constantly improving our systems here. I'm never stuck enough to say, "This is the be-all, end-all. This is the best version possible." We are always leveling up and changing, but I know to do great things together as a team, I have to make sure we are all lined up. If we're running a relay and you're running the track backward, you're gonna hand off the baton to the wrong person. We're gonna end up getting disqualified. We have to let everybody know which direction we're running and at what point they are supposed to hand off the baton, etc. We've created that expectation.

My employees show up to work over here for me. They know what they need to be clear on and what needs to be done for the day because we've had the daily and weekly meetings to keep them in line. It's been drilled into their heads. No exceptions, no excuses, over and over, time and time again. If you asked anybody who works for me, what needs to be done, they'd let you know straight up, in a heartbeat, the goals of the business.

Chapter 27: Corp Structure

Our corporate structure has what we call a pecking order, or hierarchy. One of the things that makes me angry is when I get sideswiped, or what we refer to in the office as "ambushed." I'll be the first to admit I can become angry easily. I'm passionate, and I don't like to be taken from my focus. I have Attention-Deficit Disorder due to psychological matters, but I do not take medicine for it. Instead, I have trained my brain to focus. If somebody interrupts that focus, it fucks me up and makes me angry.

I understand one of the biggest sources of my anger comes from frustration and the biggest source of frustration comes from lack of focus or not being able to focus on my goals. That said, I had to create a corporate structure that supported keeping everybody away from me as much as possible, so I could focus on my goals. It works like this. I have several different gatekeepers.

As you know, we have three divisions: the acquisition team, the money team, and the success team. The acquisition team consists of a vice president and some employees. The success team consists of an operations manager and some employees, and the money team consists of a general manager and some employees. Each division has its own gatekeeper. The vice president is the gatekeeper of the acquisition team; the operations manager is the gatekeeper for the success team, and the general manager is the gatekeeper for the money team.

These three people report to me. Jose, the GM, Lindsay, the operations manager, and Pat, the vice president all report to me and only to me. They don't report to each other. They're not held accountable by anybody other than me and themselves. However, the employees they manage are directly responsible for reporting to them and answering to them and if it's something that needs to be addressed by me, one of those three people bring it my way. When I show up here in the office, nobody is knocking on my door. Everybody leaves me the fuck alone. Nobody comes and bothers me or tries to ambush me or steal my attention. They go to one of these three people who work for me, who are my gatekeepers, and those three people decide whether it's worth my time or not. Often, they can just give the answer themselves. They have the ability and power to do so.

This allows me to keep a huge amount of my focus on where it needs to be because I'm not distracted by petty commission disputes, customer complaints about a salesperson using too much pressure on them, the general manager and sales team going back and forth (because those guys can be awfully cunning and convincing), or the success team's inability to keep up with the clients. I don't hear about any of that. I stay in my own little bubble in my own little zone making it rain over here at Break Free Academy.

That's what the CEO does. People say the CEO should know the janitor just as much as the vice president. I think that's bullshit. The CEO shouldn't know the janitor and the janitor's problems because then he's thinking about the janitor's problems instead of thinking about the company and the company's problems.

This morning, when I was at CrossFit, I had to ask what a couple of exercise moves looked like, and I had to explain that I was out of room in my brain. As a result, I had to dump some of the CrossFit exercises from my memory to stuff in some of the other information I needed to retain. Having experienced that, how can the CEO of a company like General Electric be concerned with the janitor? Sure, he should be empathetic and care about the janitor. He's a person helping to support the company. But at the same time, if you had to carry the weight of the janitor's problems, the vice president's problems and your employee's problems, you would be distracted, and your focus wouldn't be where it needed to be to run your company.

I have gatekeepers even though I only have 15 total employees. These gatekeepers run defense on every single one of them. By running defense, I mean they keep them from coming to me. They keep me focused. They keep me in the zone and from dealing with petty distractions. At any given moment, if you ask me everything is perfect. You might ask my general manager, and he'd tell you the world is falling apart out there, but that's his problem to fix. My job is to stay in my own bubble, and I hired him as a problem solver. I also compensate him heavily because of that. I overpay all my people because I'm looking for loyalty and I believe that if you pay people what they're worth, they'll give you what you want. If I want them to work really hard and I pay them what they're worth, then that's what they'll fucking do. I just wrote a bonus check to my vice president last week. It's bigger than any bonus check I've ever written to myself. Why? Because he does the work.

These gatekeepers run another kind of defense, too. They run a client defense. I'm in a lifestyle business. We have 170,000 fans on Facebook, 26,000 fans on Instagram, 10,000 followers on LinkedIn, 13,000 followers on Twitter, and the list goes on and on and on. Such as 250,000 visitors a month to our blog, a million views a week on Facebook. On YouTube, we've got 10,000 subscribers, and again, the list continues. When you have that kind of exposure, it's a certainty that a percentage of the marketplace will not like you. A percentage of the marketplace who buys your shit simply won't fucking jive with it.

Some people get mad that I cuss. Some people get mad that my shit won't work for them because they're lazy. Some people get mad because I have a faux hawk in some of my videos. Some people get mad because I drive nice cars. Some people get mad because I have a hot wife. Some people get mad because I educate my kids at an early age. When you have 1,000 friends on Facebook, if one or two annoy you, it's not that big of a deal, but when you have 100,000 fans on Facebook and 500 or 5,000 of them annoy you, it starts to add up quick. In my case, it was driving me fucking nuts. I would see people trolling my posts or people Photoshopping dicks next to my face and experience all the shit that happens when you're in the public eye. All the shit that happens from people who have never even bought my stuff and who don't know me. They just see me on the Internet and decide I'm a scumbag. I used to take that shit to heart.

Again, just like not knowing the janitor's problems allows you to grow the company faster, not knowing that trolls hate you allows you to keep your focus and grow faster as well. I put these gatekeepers in charge of dealing with the trolls, too. I don't check messages on Facebook anymore. I don't reply to comments and block and delete people myself. If someone sends us a fucked-up email, I don't read it. It goes directly to another department, to one of my managers. If someone does some shady shit, which happens often (not clients but regular people do shady shit), I don't hear anything about it.

If one of the clients goes rogue, I don't hear anything about it. I stay in my bubble because the gatekeepers run defense to make sure I can remain in my zone—and by zone—I mean comfort zone. From comfort comes clarity. I'm not referring to living your life in your comfort zone. The comfort zone allows you to operate comfortably no matter how stressful the situation. I've tried to remove as much stress as possible off my shoulders and put it on the shoulders of the people I count on and who I compensate for handling matters for me.

Because of the gatekeepers and running defense, our corporate structure is set up perfectly allowing me to stay in my bubble which keeps me happy. When I'm happy, I create happy content, and when I create happy content, people soak it up, and when people soak it up, they send us their money.

Chapter 28: Upper Limits

At this point, my company has an amazing corporate structure; we are an incredible company making money; we have gatekeepers; we have the teams lined up that we need. Everybody is doing what they're supposed to. They're in their own lane, in their own zone, and I'm over here happy.

What's next?

Some people would say that you have it all, right? You've got the right corporate structure. You've got people in line with you. You've got the meetings lined up. You've got loyal employees. What else could you want? As a business owner, I'm telling you, there's never enough. No matter if you make $10,000 a month, or $10,000,000 a month, you're gonna hit your limits. And I've had to push through a lot of upper limits as I made the transition from salesman to CEO. You see when you're a salesman, and you make $20,000 a month, you learn to live on $20,000 a month. When you're in a corporation, and you make $500,000 a month, you learn you love the potential of earning so much that you have to strive for a million. It's completely different, drawing money as a salesman from a business versus managing the business' money as a CEO.

I had some huge upper limits. I worry about taxes a lot. So, I save a lot of money for tax purposes, because it seems like you never know what those fuckers are gonna bill you until it's too late. I've had some high, high credit card bills, some six-figure American Express bills and Amex only allows you to pay things off in a month, so I've had months where I've had to stroke six-figure checks for credit card payments. At one time in my life, not too long ago, I wasn't even making $100,000 a year. Now, to be able to stroke a check in a month, or a draft from our bank in a month's time for what used to take me a year to earn is some shit that I had to mentally get over and process. As a salesman, if I'm making $100,000 a month, I'm rich as fuck. We're talking horse farms, Learjets... A hundred grand a month as a salesperson is balling.

A hundred grand a month as a business owner may just be scraping by, depending on how many employees you have, your overhead costs and your hard operating costs. The tax man and everybody else shows up. It's not always rainbows and sunshine when you're making the transition from the sales mentality to the CEO mentality. I had to push through my upper limits. First, I didn't want to hire people because when I saw $100,000 a month going out to payroll, I freaked the fuck out. The first time I saw those numbers, I fired a bunch of people, thinking *we can't have $100,000 a month going out in payroll*. Then my staff reminded me, we're making $300,000 a month, so profit after paying taxes is about $100,000 monthly for the company—which means, we were still doing okay hiring these people.

Payroll scared the hell out of me. The first time we had $150,000 in a month on the payroll, we were still in the fish hook. I thought we were going to die. I thought that was the end of it; all the savings were gone. We might as well wrap it up, pack it up, ship it, go home. But somehow, we pulled through it. We actually had money left over. The next payroll period, we had money left over, too. I've learned that even though I overcompensate my people, they always make up for it. I've had to bust through the upper limit and learn to trust them, I've had to learn that high credit card bills mean investments are coming back to us. I now understand that huge payroll means money's been made. And it's scary investing, you know?

Investing $100,000 into your employees on a monthly basis and $100,000 into advertising, bills, and operations, not counting rent, furniture, electricity, overhead time, plane tickets, hotel rooms, contractors and all the other necessities that come from running a business is terrifying. It's one thing to say Break Free Academy's making $1M a month, but it's another when you're going through a fish hook, making $1M a month and it costs you $999,000 to keep it going.

I'm not saying that's the case of my business now. We operate at a great margin. However, it has been the case before. As we've pulled out of the fish hook, over the last year, I've been fortunate enough to have quite a bit of excess money. And so, I've had to push through another upper limit, which is investing the company's money. It does no good for your company's money to sit there. If you have three months of operating capital, put that into an account, where you keep your tax money. When you funnel that into a separate account, then you pay your employees and everything else the money that's left over, the money the typical business owner puts into their own personal bank account.

But by the time you've taken the money of the company and put it in your personal bank account, you've been personally taxed on it. What I prefer to do is take that money and invest it. I've bought other corporations. I've invested in housing, flips. I've invested in land development deals, I have invested in technology companies, I have invested so many different ways. And I've written six, and multiple six-figure checks, for each of these investments because I don't want the money just sitting around. If I can give somebody $150,000 and they can come back to me with $200,000 by the end of the year, then guess what? All the sudden I've got $50,000 that I've made on that money that I loaned out and I'm not personally taking that money; the corporation loaned it out. So, if they don't pay me back in that year, then it's less money that I actually pay income taxes on because the money isn't income. It was money that came to the company and then was reinvested into the growth of the company. I won't be taxed on the gains until the next year.

You should always consult a CPA or tax attorney, who can give you legal advice on your taxes and money. I'm obviously not licensed in any of those areas, but I've had to learn to make the scary investments because our business is growing. As I invest, I also have to make sure I've protected the business by diversifying into stocks and bonds, real estate deals, company mergers, acquisitions, and all the opportunities that matter. A lot of people make the main thing the only thing, and that is a mistake. I've got to make sure if the sales training world slows up for whatever reason, and funnels are no longer required, if we're not ahead of the game, then we're diversifying and playing in multiple games at once. That is good enough to keep me happy.

Chapter 29: Replace Yourself

One of the biggest upper limits I struggled to bust through was replacing myself. I think I'm a little bit better at things than I actually am. Oftentimes, as a CEO or even as a salesperson, we tend to think that we're the best at our tasks. While you might be good at those roles, if you're a CEO, there are multiple departments, multiple facets, multiple things where you must excel. If you're good at multiple things, it's hard to be great at anything. So, I've had to learn to let go. When I let go of something, I totally let go of it. If I assign a job to somebody, I expect to never have to fucking mention that job ever again.

Nowadays, instead of just looking for ways to grow in profitability and everything else, as a CEO, I look for ways to do less and less. Just yesterday, I took my MacLaren over to my vice president's penthouse, picked him up and we had a couple of drinks and lunch at one of the nicest, hottest spots in Dallas. Beautiful people were all around us dancing and having a great time, and the food was wonderful. He said, "You know what I've noticed about you, Stewman? You are doing less and less and less in this company." He didn't say it in a negative way. The tone of his voice told me he admired what I've started doing. "You're putting the right people like me in the right places, so it frees you up to do whatever you're better at which is to strategize and put things together."

The more and more I replace myself and hire out, the more profitable we get. I asked one of my very wealthy, very successful business owner friends what he spent the majority of his time doing every day. Before he answered me, he said, "I don't know what you spend the majority of your time doing every day." I replied, "Working." He said, "You're doing it wrong. I spend the majority of my time every day thinking." He said, "We get paid to think as CEOs. Employees work. CEOs think and strategize and then have others execute." My friend's name is Dustin Black. The advice Mr. Black gave me changed my life. I started thinking how could I hire out? How could I hire people to do things for me? How could I outsource what I needed to?

Since that conversation, I've been outsourcing more and more. I've earned more and more. Every time I give up a job, more money seems to come in because I may have been good at funnels, but I wasn't the best in the world at funnels. Now, I have the person who is the best in the world working for me. It's all he focuses on, so now, our funnels are better than ever. I'm a good writer, but I'm not the best writer. Now that I have a full-time editor who is the best editor, my writing went up tenfold two years ago. All I have to do is worry about banging out rough drafts. I'm not the best at managing money, so I hired a CFO. We outsource it. All our accounting is done by Fully Accountable, a company my friend Vinnie Fisher owns. You can go to FullyAccountable.com. They send us reports, run all our numbers, tell me everything I need to know regarding the eight companies I own.

Ultimately, my next move in this company is to hire a CEO. Then I'll truly just be a business owner. I'll upscale this business all the way up from being the salesman, the service provider and everything in between to even outsourcing and hiring a CEO to replace me. Guess what? If I identify as a salesperson, chances are I'm not going to make the best CEO, and I'm fully aware of that. It's not an ego thing. It's not that I have to be in control of my company. I'm here to change lives and profit from my businesses. Nothing more, nothing less. If someone can step into the role of CEO and do it better than me and make the company more profitable, by all means, have at it. More profitability for this company simply means that we change more lives and that's what I'm all about.

As you've read this book so far, you've thought about scaling from a sales position I'm sure. Maybe you're already a CEO and are wondering how to scale to be a better CEO or how to scale yourself out of the tasks you are doing that CEOs shouldn't do. I want you to think about finding somebody else to replace you in your CEO position and ultimately, in all your jobs. You'll never truly enjoy the fruits of your labor and the benefits of your hard work if you don't start putting people into the places in your organization where they can best serve you and take the brunt of the hard work off your shoulders.

Chapter 30: Enjoy the Fruits of Scaling a Business

First, welcome to the last chapter of the book. I want to congratulate you because a lot of people pick up books, a lot of people listen to books, but they never fucking make it through the whole thing, and they quit. Just like that entrepreneurial ADD that I've talked about several times throughout the course of this book, a lot of people struggle with reading books, too. They'll get 85 percent of the way through and never finish it. If you're reading this chapter, give yourself a pat on the back, give yourself a hand, or a high five. You're one of the few people who actually finish what you start. As I've said, as a person who identifies as a salesperson but who's now sitting in a CEO role, I'm a closer and closers finish what they start.

Closers close. That's what it means. They get the deal done, and you finished this book. If you're growing a business, you've got to finish your business just the way you've finished this book. In the previous chapter, we talked about outsourcing and hiring, but then what? If you've gotten to a level where you can enjoy and spend most of your time thinking, then you can enjoy the fruits of your labor, like my friend, Dustin Black said. Dustin has a CEO for his company. He's already made the transition I haven't made yet. Bill Gates has a CEO for his company. Google has a CEO for its company, and the role was not given to any of the founders.

I want you to think about this. When you find that CEO and you can spend the majority of your time thinking, the majority of your time thinking doesn't have to be spent thinking in an office. The majority of your time thinking doesn't have to be spent thinking at home. You can think on vacations. You can think on tropical islands. You can think while being piss drunk in the Bahamas. That's why you've worked all those years. That's why you scaled the business. That's why you made the sales you did, so you can move the scales up. I know a lot of us say *I'll never quit working*. I'm not here to tell you to quit working. But, when working is thinking, and you can do thinking from anywhere, work and relaxation can become one.

As I've mentioned in previous chapters, you need the ability to operate under extremely stressful situations from the same zone of comfort that you would feel as if you were sitting on the couch flipping channels on the TV. You need the capacity to think, and you can't think under pressure. You can't think under an amazing amount of stress unless you can remove the stress from your life. Who's to say that taking a trip to Hawaii for a month at a time, maybe two months at a time, to think about and strategize your business would not be beneficial for you when you come back? Who's to say that that's not working? Who's to say that while you're up on a surfboard, you're not thinking about work? Who's to say that while you're eating the finest fish caught from the Pacific Ocean that you're not strategizing on how you could be more profitable or what employees you can lift up or what compensation you can give to people who are doing a good job?

There's no limit. That's what scaling is about. Scaling doesn't mean just making more money. Scaling is about making more money, working less, and bringing joy to yourself for the fruits of your labor and your hard work. It's not easy to read business books. Plenty of thrillers are a lot more fun to read, but you took the time to make it through this book. A lot of people create businesses, and they never scale them. We see small business owners every day. You go to the local dry cleaner, and the guy who owns it is the guy who checks in your clothes. If you went to the convenience store in the hood where I lived, the guy who owns the store is also the clerk.

That's not scaling a business. That's *working* at a business. You might as well be an employee, not a CEO. If you're a salesperson and you've got to show up at the office every single day and make sales, that's awesome. There's nothing wrong with that, but you need to think about the long game.

I'll finish the book with this. According to the Census Bureau, 20 percent of Americans make over $100,000 a year. It's a true 80/20 rule on full display. If you make a six-figure a year income, salary or commission, however you slice it, you're in the top 20 percent of our country. If you take it up a notch to see how many people in America make over $250,000 a year, you will find out that according to the Census Bureau, those folks make up only five percent of Americans.

Let's illustrate the 80/20 rule in effect once again because 20 percent of the folks who make over $100,000 a year go on to make multiple hundreds of thousands of dollars a year. You see, most people get comfortable. They make $100,000 owning a business, working in a job making sales. They get a $400 monthly Lexus payment and take a couple of trips to Cabo every year. They get an interest-only ARM loan on a nice house, and they live it up, immersed in debt, forced to work every single day unable to scale. If you look at the people who push past that initial $100,000 and make it to $250,000, they're the 20 percent. Those are the people who kept on pushing. They didn't get comfortable. They said a Lexus payment is nice, but what about a McLaren? If you look at the Census Bureau one more time, you'll note that of the people who make above $250,000, only one percent of Americans, or 20 percent of those earning over $250,000 make over $1M per year.

Very few people scale their business or build their business or income to over $1M a year. A lot of people drop off along the way. The reason they do is that they start thinking like an employee, they get stuck to their business, or they've not scaled in the best manner, in the way that would best serve them and their business. They've not leveraged other people. They've not invested in their people. They've not taken the time to train. They've simply taken an employee or salesperson mentality and stuck with it. You, my friend, have read this book. You now know there's a light on the other side. You now know you can scale a business. You now know you want to be in the one percent, the 20 above 20 above 20. You want to stay out of the 80 percent all around.

I thank you for reading this book. My goal in writing it was to share with you how to scale a business, for you to learn how to build a business the way you're supposed to, so you won't be stuck working in a business or being the business. The business will support itself. Take the lessons I've shared with you and the information you've learned and do not forget them. Go out and implement because that's the way you will grow and scale your business into what you envision it can be, no matter what you're doing right now. You know as well as I do that if you're reading this book, you didn't get into your line of business, so you could drive a Honda Accord, a BMW, a Lexus, a Mercedes or any other similar garden-variety car.

You got into this business, so you could buy the baddest house in the baddest neighborhood and drive the baddest cars and sport the baddest clothes and look like the baddest motherfucker in the room. You can do that by scaling your efforts.

Make sure you head over to HardcoreCloser.com. Check out all our latest blog posts and sign up to join my mastermind to get the support you need in scaling your business. I can help you build and put the strategic elements of your business into place to rocket-ship propel you into the future. Simply go to BreakFreeAcademy.com/Entourage.

Thanks again for reading, my friend.

About the Author

A BAMF, unafraid to take action, Ryan Stewman, aka the "Hardcore Closer," is a 4x bestselling author, podcaster and blogger. Best known for consulting with Alpha personality types on rapidly growing their sales via the use of powerful advertising and marketing, Ryan is a salesman turned CEO. He has not had a salaried job his entire life. He's mastered the art of super effective communication and has closed more transactions than he has time to count. With his no-BS approach to strategizing and scaling businesses, Ryan has helped high-net-worth performers adjust their business plans resulting in windfall profits.

After gaining prolific social media experience, Ryan decided to teach people from all sales fields and industries how to sell online, and Hardcore Closer was born. In the first year HC closed over $150K in gross sales; the second year HC hit over $300K, and in 2016, HC generated over $2M.

His notoriety and savage sales acumen have put him on the pages of the largest media publications on the planet. He contributes to and has been featured in *Forbes, Entrepreneur, Addicted2Success, The Good Men Project, The Lighter Side of Real Estate* and the *Huffington Post* in addition to other top-tier sites.

He states the key to his success is doing the work.

Hardcore Closer is an online learning resource for salespeople, selling e-learning products in the advertising, marketing funnel sales and social media arenas and offers personal coaching and live events. Break Free Academy is Hardcore Closer's flagship program and provides every tool needed to market businesses online and crush the competition.

Ryan was born and raised in Texas. He's a doting husband and proud father to three sons. He and his family live in Dallas.

Subscribe to his blog at www.HardcoreCloser.com

Made in the USA
Columbia, SC
16 July 2018